Women to Remember

AF437811

Preface

The world of the Old Testament is one in which women were not accorded much status. Women were considered inferior to men. Women without standing in society, such as handmaids, and the servants of the wealthy, were often required to submit to multiple rapes at their owner's command. Men allowed their concubines and daughters to be sexually assaulted and gang-raped. A man could keep numerous concubines as sexual partners and dismiss them when no longer needed. A father could sell his daughter as an enslaved person, and while an enslaved man was automatically given his freedom after six years, an enslaved woman remained enslaved forever. Women were not allowed to participate in the feasts of harvest, ingathering, and unleavened bread. They were not allowed into the priesthood. They were subjected to a lengthy investigation and invasive rituals if their husbands suspected them of having had an affair. No such practices were required for men suspected of infidelity. The rules of inheritance gave nothing to daughters. If a woman is not a virgin when married, she would be stoned to death, but men had no similar virginity requirements. Worse, a virgin woman who had been raped must marry her attacker regardless of her feelings towards the rapist. During the Second Temple period, women were not allowed to testify in court trials, go out in public, or talk to strangers. When outside of their homes, they were to be doubly veiled.

In the light of this diminished view of women, it is not surprising there is a lack of heroines in the Old Testament. Yet, from this handful of female protagonists who managed to elbow their way into the story of the Old Testament, there are a lot of life lessons that can be learned from them, from faith to love, from the meaning of commitment to the pitfalls of worldliness, from perseverance to rashness, from advocacy to selfishness. I have tried to capture some of these life lessons that I believe are significant for us today. I hope you enjoy reading these unauthorized biographic sketches. More importantly, you glean from these heroines some inspiration to help in your daily walk with God.

Richard Rupnarain, April 28, 2007

Table of Contents

Ruth
Love Conquers All
Story Text: Ruth 1:1-18

Now it came to pass in the days when the judges ruled that there was a famine in the land. And a certain man of Bethlehemjudah went to dwell in Moab's country, he, his wife, and his two sons. And the name of the man was Elimelech, and the name of his wife Naomi, and the name of his two sons Mahlon and Chilion, Ephrathites of Bethlehemjudah. And they came into the country of Moab and continued there. And Elimelech Naomi's husband died; and she was left, and her two sons. And they took to themselves wives of the women of Moab; the name of the one was Orpah, and the name of the other Ruth: and they dwelt there about ten years. And Mahlon and Chilion died also, and the woman was left without her two sons and her husband. Then she arose with her daughters-in-law, that she might return from the country of Moab: for she had heard in the country of Moab how that the LORD had visited his people in giving them food. Wherefore she went forth from the place where she was, and her two daughters in law with her; and they went on the way to return to the land of Judah. And Naomi said to her two daughters in law, Go, return each to her mother's house: the LORD deal kindly with you, as you have dealt with the dead, and with me. The LORD grant that you may find rest, each of you in the house of her husband. Then she kissed them, and they lifted up their voice and wept. And they said to her, Surely, we will return with you to your people. And Naomi said, Turn again, my daughters: why will you go with me? shall I bear more sons, that they may be your husbands? Turn again, my daughters, go your way; for I am too old to have a husband. If I should say, I have hope, if I should have a husband also tonight, and should also bear sons; Would you wait for them till they should be grown? would you restrain yourselves from having husbands? nay, my daughters; for it grieves me much for your sakes that the hand of the LORD has gone out against me. And they lifted up their voice and wept again: and Orpah kissed her mother-in-law, but Ruth cleaved to her. And she said, Behold, your sister-in-law has returned to her people, and to her gods: you go with your sister-in-law. And Ruth said, Entreat me not to leave you, or to turn away from following you: for where you go, I will go; and where you lodge, I will lodge: your people will be my people, and your God my God: Where you die, there will I die, and there will I be buried: the LORD do so to me, and more also if anything but death shall part you and me. When she saw that she was steadfastly resolved to go with her, then she ceased speaking to her.

Ruth was born and raised a Moabite. Moab was a nation that was famous for its polygamous practices and for its worship of idol god, Chemosh. As such the Moabite heritage was not one to boast about.

As far back as she could remember, her country was at perpetual war with the nation of Israel and was thus always under wrathful judgment of the Hebrew prophets (Is.51: 1-9). Little did she know she would one day be married to an immigrant Israelite named Mahlon and be instantly spliced into the genealogy of Christ. And had it not been for her ingrafting into this family Ruth would have remained unknown to sacred history, and the world would have been bereft of one of its most poignant love stories. She may verily have been the most beautiful, generous, kind, and sincere woman to grace the streets of Moab. Still, her life would not have counted with God because true recognition begins only when we are born again and grafted into the kingdom of the living God and His Christ. It is only then that we are made alive unto God. It is only then we are found. It is only then that we become children of God, heirs of the grace of life, are given an audience before the throne of grace, and experience true peace, unconditional love, and lasting joy. Only then can we be justified and saved from the wrath to come. And it is only then that we are assured of eternal life. For none but those whose robes are washed white in the blood of Christ are known of God. Though they might be mighty kings or fair princesses, if they are without God in this world, they are veiled in darkness impenetrable even to the piercing gaze of the All-seeing One. Alas! To be unknown by one's Creator is the most dreaded of human ailments. It is a life disconnected from the true Vine, a life blocked from the true Light, a life barred from the only Way, a life of hopelessness both here and beyond the grave. For without the continual work of the master Potter, the unregenerate life can never become even a shadow of its original intent. It must exist as an empty shell, a tinkling brass and sounding cymbal. It is a life void of meaning and purpose; a one-dimensional existence abandoned to the mercy of a deceitful heart and evil nature. It is a soul expatriated to the manipulative, ungodly, hedonistic, devilish, and murderous control of the prince of the power of the air, the spirit who works in the children of disobedience. Indeed then, it is not unreasonable to conclude that life under the influence of a ruinous law of sin and propelled by the raging current of an ungodly world system is a life bound for inevitable frustration in this world and doomed to ultimate destruction in the one to come.

Fortunately for Ruth, her marriage to Mahlon and concurrent grafting into the family of God insulated her from the fearful judgment that hung over the Moabite nation and reconnected her to the Vine, allowing the Divine plan for her life to be set in motion.

She would soon find out for herself that the bad things that happen to good people are within the scope of God's plan for His children to bring them to maturity and faith. While in Moab, she and Orpah, her sister-in-law, grieved the untimely passing of their young husbands. Whatever dreams and hopes they had for a better life appeared to have been buried with their husbands, for soon after the funeral service, Naomi, their mother-in-law, decided to return home to Bethlehem and suggested they might be better served if they returned to their former homes in Moab. But unlike Orpah, who jumped at the suggestion, Ruth determined to undertake the trek to Bethlehem with her mother-in-law. She had a rudimentary faith to believe that "all things work together for good to them that love God" and that though misfortune had befallen her, God was still sovereign and still able to fulfill His plan for her life. Perhaps in the household of her Hebrew in-laws, she had heard the story of Joseph - how he was sold into slavery and how he was exalted in due time because he remained faithful to God. But whatever the source of her faith, she knew returning to Moab was like a dog returning to its vomit and like a pig returning to its wallowing in the mud. Backsliding was not the answer. God did not deliver her from an idolatrous tradition to send her back into it and her determination to journey on with Naomi was proof. She believed Yahweh was well able to put together the broken pieces of her life and make another vessel that seemed fit to Him. So she submitted to the divine will and artistry and allowed the God of Israel to continue work on His masterpiece. On the other hand, Orpah bade them a hasty farewell and returned to Moab, her people, and her gods. Nothing more is said or written about her, confirming the claim that a life removed from God is cloaked in darkness.

Upon their arrival in Bethlehem, Ruth found work in the fields of a wealthy farmer named Boaz and soon after joined him in holy matrimony. Months later, she gave birth to a son who became the great grandfather of David and the great-great grandfather of Jesus Christ. Naomi thus became a proud and blessed grandmother. And that is the way this bittersweet love story ends. This ending, however, is not just for the Elimelech family but is atypical for all those who are willing to depart from the idolatrous ways of the world and submit their lives to the will of the one true God.

There are several theories on why this love story was included in the Canon of scripture. The most common one is that it is a response, more specifically a protest, against the post-exilic laws of Ezra and Nehemiah that sought to outlaw inter-marriage between returning Jews and the Gentile natives. We will touch on this subject a little later. Suffice it to say, however, that all scripture is given by inspiration of God and is profitable for doctrine and correction in righteousness. Hence, the book of Ruth is more than a protest, more than just a piece of romantic literature, and more than just a fragment of Jewish history. It is intended for our edification and example.

And so, with Ruth as our pivotal character and focus, we will proceed into the fields of the Word of God and "glean some of the sheaves that remain." We will discover many comforting and edifying truths about redemption from this drama. We will learn that salvation is an authentic, ongoing love story between God and humans. Such an understanding will help us appreciate our salvation and reciprocate the love of our heavenly Boaz and encourage those still in the idolatrous Moabs of this world to immigrate to the kingdom of Christ where they too will find true love. Follow me now into the fields!

***

Lesson 1: Salvation is a gift of grace.

Ruth was a Gentile girl under the condemnation of a Law that clearly stated: "An Ammonite or Moabite shall not enter the congregation of the Lord" (Deuteronomy 23: 3). Not only was she allowed to enter the congregation of the Lord, but she was escorted to the front of the redemptive line. And perceptibly so, she did not think she deserved that blessing because of her sacrifices. Instead, she rightly attributed all of it to grace – God's unmerited favor. When Boaz encouraged her to remain in his field, she humbly replied, "Why have I found grace in your eyes, that you should take knowledge of me, seeing I am a stranger?"(2: 10).

Ruth's response is a timely reminder to a world that mistakenly believes in justification by works of righteousness. Scripture makes it clear that "all have sinned and come short of the glory of God," and that there is none good, not even one person. To add salt to the wound, Jeremiah condemned our righteousness as "filthy rags," and Isaiah diagnosed our condition as being sick in the head and faint in the heart, "even from the sole of the foot." This is certainly not the kind of diagnosis that religious people like to hear. Nevertheless, it is the unconditional verdict of God on human depravity. All without exception have sinned, and all are therefore sinners. And, just as a dirty fountain cannot bring forth clean water, the sin-tainted nature cannot produce works free from impurities. This universal depravity also explains why even the most pious of people, with all their noble intentions, cannot redeem their fellow humans and why the substitutionary death of Christ on the cross was necessary. Paul concurred: "For he [God] has made him [Christ] to be sin for us, who knew no sin; that we might be made the righteousness of God in him" (2Corinthians 5: 21). Sinful humans needed a sinless redeemer, and God provided that Savior in Christ the Lord.

The church is not excluded from the charge of falling prey to the bewitching instinct in human nature that says we can merit or earn our salvation. Those at Galatia felt this way and for this reason, were sharply rebuked by Paul:

> O foolish Galatians, who has bewitched you, that you should not obey the truth, before whose eyes Jesus Christ has been evidently set forth, crucified among you? This only would I learn of you, did you receive the Spirit by the works of the law, or by the hearing of faith? Are you

so foolish? Having begun in the Spirit, are you now made perfect by the flesh?" (Galatians 3: 1-3).

Paul explained that if people could be saved by the steadfast observance of laws and commandments, then the cross of Christ was meaningless.

> Therefore, he says, "I do not frustrate the grace of God, for if righteousness comes by the law, then Christ died in vain (Galatians 2:21).

Two thousand years later, non-Christian traditions still need to be reminded that salvation is a free gift of God - for by grace are we saved. Today many sincere people mutilate their bodies, hoping to win divine empathy. Some practice a life of asceticism while others continue to offer empty sacrifices, hoping to find justification with God. Likewise, the Church needs a reminder that it is grace by which we continue our walk with God. On the other hand, many Christian believers are convinced that if they enter a prolonged period of fasting and prayer or discharge their financial obligations to the church or attend the house of the Lord regularly, they become eligible for divine favor. Albeit subtly so, both groups, sinners, and saints alike, are under the charming influence of the lie that says our works of righteousness can justify us. But as we meditate on the redemption of Ruth, we are made conscious once again of the efficacy and the all-sufficient power of grace to save to the uttermost them that call on the Lord:

> For by grace are ye saved through faith; and that not of yourselves: it is the gift of God: not of works, lest any man should boast (Ep.2:8, 9).

Like Ruth, we will be spared from tedious and fruitless strivings when we learn that salvation is not earned but that it is received by faith. We will learn that it is not self-righteous works that will position us for divine approbation and advancement in the kingdom of God but the grace of God. By faith Ruth received this gracious offer from Boaz and by faith we must receive the grace of God that is made available in Christ.

Lesson 2: We must encourage backsliders to return to the house of God.

The story commenced with the family of Elimelech living in Bethlehem, "the house of Bread." They left Bethlehem for the prosperous Moab at the threat of impending famine. While there, divine judgment visited them and took the lives of the menfolk in its wake. This domestic crisis, coupled with an economic downturn in Moab, forced them to return to Bethlehem, and there, the blessings of God returned to them with such surprising quickness that they had little time to mope the tragedy of the terrible years in Moab.

This tragedy of unbelief and triumph of faith serves both as a warning against apostasy and encouragement to dissidents of the faith to return to the fold from whence they have strayed. It warns the prodigal sons and daughters who take for granted the comforts and security of salvation in the Father's house and arrogantly defect for what appears to be greener pastures that if they are away from the protection and guidance of the Father, it is only a matter of time before they are quickly overtaken by moral famine and spiritual deprivation. Before they know it, they will find themselves lonely, needy, morally, and financially bankrupt, and forced to live on the refuse of pigs. They will quickly learn that the way of the backslider is hard. Such was the experience of the family of Elimelech. Fortunately, it is often at this point of emptiness and brokenness that backsliders usually come to their senses. Their sense of awareness is heightened, and they begin to see things from a more enlightened perspective. Armed with a solid point of reference to assess their present position, the backslider is made painfully aware of the actual value of what was forfeited and the uselessness of what was gained in that poor exchange. They will suddenly realize that even "my father's servants have more to eat than I." But it is also at this point, the crisis of soul becomes more acute, and the decision of destiny hangs precariously in the balance. The forces of evil begin to circle like vultures, poised for battle against the hosts of heaven. While the Spirit of the Lord woos the heart, Satan stymies the backslider with lies. Only losers return, he says. Be a man and stick it out, he says. They will laugh at you, he says. You will fall away again, he discourages. Undoubtedly, many questions flooded the minds of these returning women. What will others say? Will the townsfolk despise us? But despite fighting within and fears without, the strong will return to the Father's house. Naomi was determined to return home and to start over, even if it meant being at the bottom of the social ladder.

However, to their surprise, they were given a warm and hospitable reception, and so too will all those who once knew Christ but who have since been lured into the idolatrous and sensuous Moabs of the world. Perhaps you have painfully experienced the emptiness, heartbreak, and broken dreams the world had to offer, and you now know the dark side deceived you. Now that you have come to your senses arise from self-loathing, shake the dust of the past off and set your face like a flint to the community of faith. God has overruled the events of your life to bring you to this point because He loves you. In the epistle to the Hebrews, the writer comforted the suffering Hebrews with this encouragement: "Whom the Lord loves, those he will chasten" (Heb.12:6).

Christians are not illegitimate children but adopted sons and daughters of our heavenly Father, and like any good father, God will chastise His children for righteousness' sake. Hence your return to the Lord should not be driven by guilt or shame but instead be constrained by the knowledge that God loves you. Naomi and Ruth returned, and as soon as they were reconnected with the community of faith, the blessings of the Lord resumed its natural flow into their lives.

Backsliders, if you reconnect your life to the righteous Branch its divine sap will resume its flow into your life. Therefore, come back to Bethel, the "house of bread," and let God end the spiritual famine in your life.

Lesson 3: Live virtuously - regardless of the moral condition of the times.

Ruth's godly life and conduct are strong proof that it is possible to live pleasing to God even within the ambiance of immorality and godlessness. Ruth lived during the period of the Judges, a time framed in moral bankruptcy and spiritual depravity. This period extended for some 400 years and was very much a time when every man and woman did what was right in their own eyes. While men in leadership positions, like judge Gideon, took to themselves many wives, others like Samson, the judge whose sexual promiscuity blends his name with Delilah, yoked themselves with the heathen. Yet, despite the moral laxity of their time and the poor example set by leadership, Ruth remained pure and unblemished. In the end, she was greatly rewarded in that she found favor with God.

The Woman's Bible makes the entry that Ruth emulated the character of the virtuous woman as described by Solomon in Proverbs 31, in that others recognize her commitment to family (Ruth 2:11,12; Prov.31:11,12); she provides sustenance for her household (Ruth 2:14, 18; Prov.31: 15); she pays attention to her appearance (Ruth 3:3,5; Prov.31:22); her manner of selfless living won the praise of many (Ruth 2:11; Prov.31:28); and her commitment to God was unquestionable (Ruth 1:16; Prov.31:30). Indeed her life argues strongly and convincingly against the lie that truth is relative. Truth cannot be relative because the truth is an immutable Person, the Lord Jesus Christ. He said, "I am the Way, the Truth, and the Life (John 14:6), meaning He is not just a teacher or a revealer or a representative of truth, but the embodiment of truth. If Ruth believed that truth was relative, she could undoubtedly have justified a sinful life on the ground that everyone did what was right in their own eyes, even the Judges who ruled in that period. Or following the example of many people who have resorted to acts of immorality to make ends meet, Ruth could have pressed her case on the ground that she was widowed at a young age and was forced to provide for herself in a patriarchal society. But as far as she was concerned, none of those reasons were justifiable, and there was no excuse for immoral living.

Without a doubt, the desire for righteous living is severely impaired when there is pervasive societal lawlessness. Widespread immorality takes the pressure off an individual to cease personal corruption. Pervasive lawlessness also appeases the individual conscience by searing it with the prevarication that the majority is always right.

This is where the logic of numbers is challenged. Truth is immune to numbers. If everyone agrees that the sun rises in the west, they will still be wrong. The degree to which truth is revealed may vary with the amount of light available. But the truth remains the truth. Thus, when Jesus claims to be the Truth and warns that the way to hell is broad and the gate to destruction is wide and is traveled by many, His warning must be heeded because it is true (Mt.7:13,14).

Another factor that restrains virtuous living is economic status. The poor contend it is difficult to survive by being totally honest. The rich, on the other hand, can hardly be spoken of in the same sentence with virtue. The generation of wealth is associated with a certain degree of dishonesty, and it produces people that are mostly arrogant and indifferent to the plight of the poor and the unfortunate. So everyone has their excuse for not being able to maintain integrity. But in the account of Ruth and Boaz, both individuals are described with the same Hebrew term *hayil,* which describes a noble character or standing. One is male, the other female. One is a native Israelite, the other a despised foreigner. One is old, the other young. One is wealthy, the other poor. The conclusion is indisputable: Virtue in living is independent of economic, cultural, age and gender issues.

Another charge against virtuous living is that there is no benefit because righteous acts go unnoticed and without reward. At the same time, evil people and their wickedness seem to prosper. The statement that it does not pay to live righteously is not uncommon. Even the psalmist was forced to ponder the fortune of the wicked and the apparent destitution of the righteous. However, he concluded that the righteous would flourish like the palm tree and grow like Lebanon's cedar (Psa.92:12). In other words, it is how the story ends that matters and the end of the righteous is always rewarding. This is because God sees and takes notes. His eyes go to and fro the ends of the earth beholding the works of the children of men (2Chron.16:9). This is the testimony of scripture. While the rest of the world was indifferent to the need for sober and godly living, God saw Noah, a righteous man, and delivered him from the universal Flood judgment. God saw righteous Lot vexing his soul amidst the perversity of Sodom and delivered him before the destruction of the city. He saw Mary, the young virgin who kept herself pure, and selected her to be *Theotokos*, the Mother of God. He saw virtuous Ruth and wedded her to Boaz. He saw Hagar alone in the wilderness dying and saved her life. So while no other person may take notice of your virtuous life, rest assured God does, and contrary to the poet who says that the good that men do is oft interred with their bones, the hour comes when God will acknowledge your life of virtue and exalt you to the highest place. The good of the righteous will live and forever be a trophy in honor of their goodness.

We also see Ruth's integrity in marriage. She was married to Mahlon, whose name means "sickly," and who it appears was sickly for most of his life. Yet, despite life's hand, she did not attempt to justify any extra-marital relationships or press a divorce case. Instead, she remained faithful to her marriage vow to stay with her husband "in sickness and health, until death does us part." Her ultimate triumph then is the triumph of virtue over vices and good over evil. Every attempt to justify sinful and immoral living today must concede in the light of her victory.

Lesson 4: Love conquers all.

Ruth was a Moabite, a descendant of Moab, the son of Lot's incestuous union with his eldest daughter after their flight from Sodom (Genesis 19:37). This is no enviable ancestry. Consider today how one is made to feel when they are conceived out of wedlock. They are called illegitimate children. Now imagine how a Moabite would feel when their names are always appended with the words "the Moabite." The awareness of an incestuous heritage is always stirred up in the consciousness. In fact, Ruth herself is often addressed in this story as Ruth the Moabite. To make matters even worse, Moab had become a "thorn in the side" of Israel when they retreated at Kadesh-Barnea. And to crown it off, there was even a prophecy that indicated the destruction of the Moabite nation when the "Star out of Jacob" comes (Numbers 24:17). Yet, even though Ruth was a member of a despised race on the brink of sure annihilation, she was spared and grafted into the vine in a most intimate and enviable manner through the power of love. She destroyed the myth that there is no hope for complete deliverance from bondage to generational maledictions.

I love to recount the story of the Samaritan woman who was married several times and lived promiscuously and how Jesus lifted the curse from her life and transformed her into a flaming evangelist. Also, that of the woman who was caught in the act of adultery and awaiting death at the hands of angry villagers and religious hypocrites, and how Jesus silenced her accusers, forgave her sin and released her from a life of immorality. These women and countless others experienced the liberating power of Christ to break the constraints of deep-rooted evils.

Indeed, the love of Jesus is immeasurably wonderful! As the song says, "So high, you can't get over it. So wide, you can't get around it. So low, you can't get under it. Love. Wonderful love!" Jacob, the deceiver, will testify that there is no one so steeped in sin that they cannot be reached by the extended arms of God's love and be elevated to princely power with God and men. Saul, the destroyer, will affirm that there is no sin too great for the love of God to forgive. The woman caught in the act of adultery will assure us there is no life too messed up for the love of God to restore. And Ruth will graciously tell us that the incomprehensible love of God overcomes racial and religious obstacles and brings anyone who so desires into the heart of the program of God. Behold, what manner of love the Father has bestowed on us that we should be called the children of God! Take heart then, friend, for there is no sin too resilient for the power of grace divine to break, and no vice so inveterate that mercy is rendered impotent to uproot, and no transgression that surmounts the apex of divine forgiveness, for "where sin abounds grace does much more abound."

So do not surrender to the lie that your script has been written and that it cannot be changed. Stop excusing wrongful living on the ground of inherited curses. And stop blaming your heritage. Your parents had their share of problems and inherited distresses as well. Going back to Adam and Eve, every household can talk about problems and curses. But the love of God is redemptive. It can reverse all harmful addictions and maledictions. So ask Him to shed that divine love into your heart and see the difference it will make in your life (Rom.5:5). Ruth's redemption confirms there is no curse the power of divine love cannot break.

Lesson 5: Commitment to godly living requires moral and mental toughness.

The narrator informs us that Orpah agreed quickly to the suggestion that it might be advantageous for her to return to Moab and that she made a hasty exit for her former homeland. She was unwilling to undertake the journey of faith because it was an unnecessary risk as far as she was concerned. On the other hand, Ruth was prepared to abandon everything for the knowledge of the one true God. She left her country and friends and joined Naomi in searching for that goodly pearl. Dr. Don Leggett observed that, from a cultural perspective, Ruth had chosen death over life. She disavowed the solidarity of the family. She abandoned her national identity. She renounced religious affiliation. In the entire epic of Israel, notes Leggett, only Abraham matches this radicality, but then he had a call from God (Gen.12:1-5). It was a divine promise that motivated and sustained his leap of faith. Besides, Abraham was a man with a wife and other possessions to accompany him. Ruth stood alone. She possessed nothing. No God has called her. No deity has promised her blessing. No human has come to her aid. She lives and chooses without a support group, and she knows the fruit of her decision may well be the emptiness of rejection and death.

Like her, those who choose to follow the Lord will soon find it is not a leisurely pursuit. Like Moses, some will be required to relinquish prestigious positions in this world and suffer the reproaches of Christ so that others might be "drawn out" from the kingdom of darkness. Or, like Abraham, some may be called upon to leave their country and their kin for the sake of the gospel and sojourn in a strange land all the days of their lives. Or, like Matthew, some may be required to leave their occupation to follow the Lord (Lk.5:27, 28). Or, like Peter, the commitment to Christ may demand severing ties with family and friends (Mk.10:28). Or, like Paul, some may be required to count their intellectual gains and achievements as dung to apprehend Christ (Phil.3:8). As Dietrich Bonhoeffer, the German theologian, insisted, there is cheap and costly grace, and the latter is the price of discipleship.

Of course, the devil will attempt to deter many a seeker from committing to Christ by projecting the Christian experience as a life marked only by reproach, denials, testing, and trials. He will call to mind all the "pleasures of sin" that one must sacrifice to make a genuine commitment to Christ. But he will conceal from them the ultimate truth about sin, that it is temporal and superficial, and that its fruit is eventual death. On the other hand, he conceals the whole truth about suffering for righteousness. He does not disclose that those who suffer along with Christ will also reign with Him and that those who deny selfish pursuits for the gospel will obtain a far greater reward than this world has to offer. Jesus, on the other hand, makes an open offer to all humanity and has no hidden agenda. All those who "will come after" Him must deny themselves, take up their cross and follow Him. But they will be compensated. They will receive a hundredfold blessing in this life and eternal life in the world to come (Matt.19:29). The outcome of the story of Ruth is a concurring testimony to this truth. She committed herself in reckless abandon to the decree of faith and was recompensed immeasurably more than she sacrificed. She came into the blessings of the covenant people, married happily to a man who loved her and provided well for her needs, became the mother to Obed, and great grandmother to Jesus - a hundredfold recompense for her selfless surrender to the call of God.

A few years ago, a terminally ill minister penned these words in his diary shortly before going to his Maker: "For me to live is Christ and to die is gain. No way to lose!" How true! St. Paul agreed that even our adversities work for our advantage. He wrote: "For our light affliction, which is but for a moment, works for us a far more exceeding and eternal weight of glory" (2Corinthians 4: 17).

Ruth also reminds us that commitment is the key to all meaningful inter-personal relationships and the bedrock on which such relationships are maintained. Many Bible scholars believe that the central message of the book of Ruth is the loyalty of God that He desires to reproduce in the lives of His children by revealing the extent of His faithfulness to us and showing us the outcome when we reciprocate such loyalty to Him. How appropriate a lesson this is in a world where loyalty is a rapidly disappearing commodity. Like Judas Iscariot, many betray their best friends for a few pieces of silver, marriage vows appear to be an obsolete tradition, and parents are ushered away to retirement homes because of disloyal children. On the other hand, Ruth was willing to give up home and family to follow the one true God, and she gladly accepted a different people, in a different environment, and of another faith. Her commitment was severely tested, but it withstood the vicissitudes of life in Moab and Judah - a life shadowed by multiple deaths, widespread famine, and family separation. In her passionate clinging to Naomi (Ruth 1:14), we experience the faithfulness of God to His covenant children. Oh, that we might see the wisdom of commitment without compulsion.

Ruth teaches us one other truth about commitment: It is for the long haul. Once a vow is made to God it must be kept to the very end. As soon as she chose the God of Naomi, her faith was immediately tested by an inducement to return to "her gods" (1:15). Orpah was given the same offer, and she grabbed it without a second thought. On this Radio broadcaster, Vernon McGee observed: "Orpah went back into idolatry. Nothing more is said of her...Ruth chose God, and He chose her in the greatest plan of the ages: namely, the bringing of Jesus Christ into the world. Ruth chose God when she chose to go with Naomi. She never stood again at the crossroads of life to decide for eternity" (*The Romance of Redemption*).

Likewise, those willing to share in "all spiritual blessings in heavenly places in Christ Jesus" must be prepared to share in His sufferings. They must carefully count the cost of commitment and live for Christ with all the energies of heart and soul. They must be ready and willing to make a joyful choice for Christ and His people regardless of the spiritual condition of the Church. They must resolve to continue in the faith and persevere despite setbacks, and their allegiance to Christ must be more robust than that which kept Ruth and Naomi inseparable. Nothing but death would separate them, and nothing but death must separate us from our commitment to Christ. And as they bound their souls together with a promise never to break their commitment to each other, we must bind ourselves to Christ with a promise never to break our commitment to the gospel and His kingdom. As they cleaved to each other, we must cleave to Christ, and as the two became one in the soul, we must also become one with Christ. As Ruth and Naomi pledged to remain faithful to each other until "death parts you from me" (Ruth 1:16), Jesus expects the Christian to be "faithful unto death" (Rev.2:10). Matthew Henry agrees:

> When we take God for our God, we must take His people for our people in all conditions; though they are a poor despised people, yet if they be His, they must be ours. Having cast in our lot among them, we must be willing to take our lot with them and to fare as they fare. We must submit to the same yoke and draw in it faithfully, take up the same cross and carry it cheerfully, go where God will have us to go, though it should be into banishment, and lodge where He will have us to lodge, though it be in a prison, die where he will have us to die, and lay our bones in the grave of the upright, who enter into peace and rest in their beds, though they be put into the graves of common people.

Such is the nature of genuine commitment. It is for the long haul - even unto death.

Lesson 6: The will of God for our lives is progressively revealed as we labor in his Kingdom.

Ruth confirms that conscientious service in the kingdom of God, irrespective of the nature of the work involved, is the vehicle by which the will of God is revealed to individuals. She labored long and difficult hours, even from "morning until evening," and was not ashamed to be seen doing menial work. Besides picking up leftovers in the fields she was forced to endure the taunts of ogling men. Yet, despite it all, she never complained but labored fervently and diligently, patiently awaiting the unfolding of the divine purpose and plan for her life.

One of the tough questions that face many Christians today is, how can I know the will of God for my life? Unfortunately, many mistakenly believe that the will of God is revealed in a vision, dream, or visitation from angels. Though God has shown His will at times in such a manner, those are rare and specific circumstances. It is not His usual mode of revelation. Mostly the will of God is revealed to us progressively as we commit ourselves to honest and diligent employment in His kingdom. What we do is not nearly as essential as our obedience and willingness to work. For as long as work is sincere and virtuous, it is dignified. As Max Ehrmann said, every job is a "real possession in the changing fortunes of time." What is vital to understand, though, is that when we are in motion, working for the Lord, we facilitate the hands of God in controlling and directing our movement, even as a driver can manipulate a moving vehicle with greater ease than he can one which has come to a dead stop. This is partly the message of the potter and the clay as found in the 18th chapter of the book of Jeremiah. The clay, representing the believer, must be mounted on the potter's wheel, spun, and chiseled so that a "vessel unto honor" might be produced. The wheel speaks of industry, diligence, and hard work. The spinning wheel speaks of motion. Thus, if we will conform to divine specifications, we must be willing to be spun and chiseled while in motion. Only then can the Potter execute His grand design for our lives. How vital then it is for us to be gainfully employed in the fields of the kingdom if we expect to know the will of God. Many complain, of course, that there is no work for them in the local church, and so they remain idle and disgruntled. The problem, however, is never a shortage of work but a lack of laborers, and one major contributor to that deficiency in labor supply is the apathy of laborers to volunteer for service, meaning that unless they are approached with an assignment, it is unlikely that they will request one. Ruth, however, almost begged for work, beseeching Boaz, "I pray thee."

Another factor contributing to the shortage of labor is general disinterestedness in tasks that appear menial. Everyone desires the work of an evangelist, a pastor, or a teacher, and if no such positions are available, they refuse to do "demeaning" work. Agreed, we may not all be gifted as a pastor, teacher, or evangelist, or there might be no such positions available, but the lack of such gifting should not prevent us from being able to convey gleanings from the Word of God to the sick and needy. For example, a little maid gleaned a few words to the wife of Naaman, the Syrian general, and saved him from the leprosy of body and soul. A little boy gleaned a few loaves and fishes to Christ and was abundantly satisfied to see the multitude fed. We may not be able to raise Lazarus from the dead, but we can help remove the stone from the tomb and unloose his bandages. In the kingdom of God, there is room for reapers and gleaners. Ruth gleaned diligently, "she came and has continued from morning until now." She made the most of each day, redeeming the time and working while it is day for "the night comes when no one can work." And she obtained the reward, for as W. M. Smith observed, "it is not genius that wins the goal, but plodding earnestness."

Regarding labor in the fields of souls, Ruth reminds us that there is work for everyone, but that work must be sought out, and when obtained, must be approached with watchful diligence and "plodding earnestness." It follows that if you are desirous of knowing the will of God for your life, and you should, you must be willing to arise from apathy and get involved in the work of the kingdom. Do anything you can for the Lord, despite how meager or menial it may appear to others. For in so doing you will facilitate the hands of Master Potter in directing you to your heavenly vocation.

Lesson 7: The just shall live by faith.

It is true that Ruth chanced upon the field of Boaz, that is, she did not predetermine which field she would glean from before leaving home that morning. Yet, her choice was not of fate, but of "faith," that God would order her steps in His way. And He did. That morning, Providence directed her steps into the fields of Boaz. And the rest is history! Dr. Leggett points out concerning the mysterious use of the word "chance" (2:3b), that there is an intentional ploy on the part of the book's writer, who calls this meeting an accident, to point out that God directs even the accidental. Often, we are apt to feel it was fate that brought us into the fellowship of Jesus Christ, a chance happening that turned out well. Not so! With God, there is no such thing as luck and chance. All things are under His control, and

His sovereign Lordship assures that all things will work together for our benefit. Thus, if Christ is not your Savior, you did not "chance upon" this book. Providence was at work on your behalf to draw you to Him. If He has brought you to a place of decision, you may choose Christ, the heavenly Boaz, and be delivered from spiritual poverty and widowhood, or you may choose to remain in spiritual poverty. That choice is yours alone. But destiny has made its offer.

As Ruth was led of faith, so too the just are saved by faith; sanctified by faith (Acts 26:18); and justified by faith (Romans 3:28). They also stand by faith (Romans 11:20); walk by faith (2Corinthians 5:7); live by faith (Galatians 2:20); overcome the world by faith (1John 5:4); and die in faith (Hebrews 11). Indeed, "without faith it is impossible to please God" (Hebrews 11:1), and equally impossible to obtain anything from Him, for he that comes to God must first believe that He is and that He is a Rewarder of those who diligently seek Him (Heb.11:6). If we live and walk by faith, as Ruth did, God will also order our steps on the path of abundant life.

Lesson 8: Jesus is all we need.

In the first conversation between Ruth and Boaz, we are reassured of the sufficiency of Christ for all our needs. Boaz, who is a type of Christ, meaning that in some respects he is an Old Testament foreshadowing of Christ, suggested to Ruth that she should "go not to glean in another field" (2: 8) since his fields were adequate for all her needs. We are reminded that we do not need to "glean in another field," for in Christ is all the fullness of the Godhead bodily, and we are complete in Him (Col.2: 9). Because of His sufficiency, saints are admonished to "love not the world, neither the things in the world" (1John 2: 15). In the fields of Christ, we will find:

- An abundance of grace (Ro.5:17).
- An abundance of love (Ep.3:19).
- Universal healing for the whole man (Isa.53:5).
- An incomprehensible peace of mind (Ph.4:7).
- Availability of continuous renewal (Isa.40:31).
- Enablement to accomplish our goals (Ph.4:13).

- Impenetrable security and constant protection (Psa.34:7).
- Fullness of joy (Jn.15:11).
- Everlasting mercy (Psa.106:1).
- An inexhaustible source of supplies (Ph.4:19).
- Deep and soothing comfort for grievous times (2Co.1:3).
- Empowerment to overcome the world system (Jn.16:33).
- Power to overcome Satan (Lk.10:19).
- Victory over the flesh (Ro.8:2-4).
- Dominion over sin (Ro.6:14).
- Abundant living in this life (Jn.10:10), and
- Eternal life in the world to come (Jn.3:16).

Why then should we glean in any other field? Jesus is all that we need. Major Ian Thomas says it best: "If you are born again, all you need is what you have, and what you have is what He is!" (*The Saving Life of Christ*). Yes, Jesus is our Sufficiency.

Lesson 9: We must be prepared to fight to secure our inheritance.

Ruth went out into the fields to glean what was left for the poor by the owners, and she gleaned diligently, continuing "even from the morning until even" to garner as much grain as she could. In this, we are reminded that even though our Boaz has bequeathed to us "exceeding great and precious promises," it is our duty to gird up the loins of our minds, put our hands to the plow, and seize our possessions. This is the principle of appropriation. Even though Israel was given the promise of Canaan, a "land flowing with milk and honey," with the assurance that "every place that the sole of your feet shall tread on would be yours," it was their duty to plant their feet on that rich land. Appropriation of the inheritance was not as easy as standing on the ground and quoting the promise of God. They must rid the land of its Canaanite dwellers through armed conflict and must guard it against the possibility of repossession.

Likewise, the promises of God, though sure, will only become the property of those willing to engage and overcome the enemy in spiritual warfare. Confession of the Word of God is not enough to materialize its promise. We must put 'foot to faith.' We must walk the talk. For faith without works is dead. It will avail nothing. As Bonhoeffer rightly observed, because Christ has purchased salvation and offered it freely to all humanity, there is the temptation to be indifferent to the need for costly discipleship. For many saints, the only obligation seems to be to go to church on Sundays and get involved in a few programs of the local community of faith. Such indifference to spiritual warfare is far from the teaching of the Bible. The New Testament writers employed terms like *fighting a good warfare, wrestling against principalities and powers, enduring hardship as a good soldier* to describe the Christian vocation. In the book of Revelation, Jesus reminded the churches that only overcomers would eat of the tree of life, be spared from the second death, eat of the hidden manna, obtain power over the nations, be clothed with white raiment, become a pillar in the temple of God, and sit with him on his throne (Rev. Ch. 2-3).

So let us arise, put on the whole armor of God, and advance into the enemy's territory. We have the assurance that we are fighting within victory and that the result of the battle is a foregone conclusion. We will overcome. Through the power of the Spirit, we will win the war and obtain the crown.

Lesson 10: God is a near and present help.

Even though Boaz was in proximity, Ruth never knew it until he revealed himself. She was oblivious to the presence of a near relative. In this, we are assured, whether we sense it or not, of the constant abiding presence of Christ. Unlike Hinduism, which teaches that God is "impersonal essence," or Buddhism, which teaches either there is no God or that he is "impersonal Buddha essence," or Islam, which teaches that God is unknowable, the Bible reveals God as a loving Creator who watches over His children with jealous care and who desires to make Himself known to them. He enjoyed regular communion with Adam and Eve in Eden until the Fall fractured their relationship. But the desire for closeness to His creation remained just as strong. So after the Fall, He instituted the Tabernacle whereby He could once again draw close to man. However, His presence was still veiled to all but the high priest. So He chose to come personally and tabernacle among humans through His Son. This time He was so close Jesus was able to declare, "He who hath seen me hath seen the Father." Still, God was not satisfied. He wanted even more intimate communion with His people, and the plan to accomplish that goal was executed upon the departure of Christ and the descent of the Holy Spirit. Through the indwelling presence of the third Person of the Godhead, saints are made into temples of the living God, and God can be with His people "always, even to the end of this age." As a result of this abiding presence:

a. We can be strong when faced with trials and adversities:

> When you pass through the waters, I will be with you; and through the rivers, they will not overflow you: when you walk through the fire, you will not be burnt; neither shall the flame kindle on you (Isaiah 43: 2).

b. We can be encouraged in the journey of life:

> And behold, I am with you, and will keep you in all places where you go and bring you again into this land; for I will not leave you until I have done that which I have declared to you (Genesis 28: 15).

c. We are assured of victory over our enemies:

> When you go out to battle against your enemies, and see horses, and chariots, and a people more than yourself, be not afraid of them: for the LORD your God is with you, who brought you out of the land of Egypt (Deuteronomy 20: 1).

d. We are assured of reward as well as judgment:

> The eyes of the LORD are in every place, beholding the evil and the good (Proverbs 15: 3).

Indeed, experience itself has taught us that Jesus Christ, the true Boaz, is always near, ready, and willing to take us to Him and to redeem His inheritance. Like the ladder to heaven that was in proximity to where Jacob fell asleep, Jesus, our Ladder to heaven, is always near at hand. Perhaps your situation appears bleak and hopeless. As you look around all you see is desolation and destitution. You stand at the crossroads of life not knowing which way to go next. You feel forsaken, deprived, cheated, and frightened, and you begin to entertain life-threatening thoughts. Yet, you must know that salvation is in proximity. Though mother and father may have left you, the Lord is ready to adopt you and make you His own. You are never alone. The eyes of your Boaz are on you, constantly, anxiously watching, and waiting for your approach. Ruth found him nearby, and if you should seek the Lord, you too will discover that "he is not far from every one of us" (Acts 17:27).

Lesson 11: We must take the initiative in reaching out to God for redemption.

I stated in the first lesson that salvation is an act of grace. By this, I mean that our self-righteous works are not saving us. We must accept the finished work of Christ as an offer of grace - the unmerited favor of God. But acceptance or rejection of that offer of grace lies within our power. It is in this sense that human initiative and response are required. In other words, faith must gratuitously shake hands with grace and receive it without proving worthiness or deservedness.

Even though Boaz secretly desired a relationship with Ruth, and even though it could be argued that he created the environment for her to see his love and experience his grace and kindness, he was not the one who initiated the marriage proposal. As strange as this practice may seem, it was not out of order with the law of redemption. The Law required the "wife of the dead" to take the initiative to let her intention be known (Deuteronomy 25: 5, 7-10), and the "redeemer" could not proceed with the act of redemption unless such intentions were unmistakably clear.

In this requirement, we are given a timely reminder that the Lord will never force Himself into a relationship with anyone but that the onus of initiating such a relationship is an individual challenge. This is not to say that grace is not at work in the unregenerate heart to move it towards God. Scripture teaches us that unless the Lord draws men and women to Himself, they cannot come to Him. And unless the Spirit reveals Christ, human hearts cannot know him. But St. Augustine and Luther have contended strongly that salvation is all of grace, to the point where it seems that the sinner has no part in the process. I disagree. If the sinner has no part in redemption, in the sense that there is no divine-human cooperation, then the sinner cannot genuinely claim to have accepted Christ as Savior. It is no longer a voluntary decision. Calvinists claim that those redeemed - the elect - have no say in the matter. Because they are elected, they must respond positively to the offer of salvation. However, Scripture presents an offer of salvation made to the whole world, which must be received by faith. Those who do not believe will perish, and those who believe in Christ will not perish but have eternal life (Jn.3:16). This is why the Gospel must be preached to the ends of the world: to give every person an opportunity for salvation. This is the consistent teaching of the New Testament. A case in point is that in which the apostle Peter attributed the delay of the return of the Lord to the longsuffering of God, who is not willing that any should perish but that all should come to repentance (2 Pet.3:9). To say that God gave His only Son for the sins of the world and that He delays the return of Christ so that everyone may be allowed to accept Christ, and then in the same breath, contend that He has elected some to salvation and some to destruction is no small charge against the integrity of a just, loving, and merciful God.

This theological position was conceived in the minds of men who thought they needed to defend the efficacy of the atoning work of Christ. The premise of the argument for election is that if all people are not saved through the atoning work of Christ, then His mission is a failure. To correct that perception, Calvinists contend that Christ died for the elect, and since the elect will be saved [an inescapable truism], the mission of Christ will ultimately be successful. This means that they base Christ's success on complete acceptance by all. It negates the fact of free will in humans. It says that humans are not free to reject God, and if they do, it is because they were not elected to salvation in the first place.

Perhaps a case study will help to elucidate the fault in this argument. Let us take Adam as our example. Adam was hand-made by God and empowered to be His vice-regent on earth. Daily, God communed with Him and his wife in the Garden of Eden. In Luke's genealogy, Adam is even called the son of God, not in being co-substantial with God, but certainly as an offspring of God. The question then is, Was Adam elected to salvation? Few would argue that he was elected to destruction and if they do, it is only *post facto* the Fall. In other words, if this question were asked to someone present before the Fall while Adam was in communion with God, the answer would be a clear, Yes. It would have been ludicrous to suggest that Adam was created to be destroyed. But then Adam disobeys God and is driven from the presence of the Lord. Is he still elected to salvation? If he never repented his sin, the Calvinists would conclude that he could not be elected. Otherwise, God would have failed in His purpose. If he repented, then he was elected to salvation. So, either way, God is saved from embarrassment. This position grants no consideration to the operation of free will in Adam. His choice to disobey God is irrelevant. He disobeyed because he was not elected to obedience. In other words, he has no choice, and he plays no part in the process. And if he plays no role in being saved, then it could be argued that he plays no role in his being lost.

While it is accepted that sinners are dead in trespasses and sins and that they need the regenerative power of the Spirit of God to draw them to God and to reveal Christ to them, Scripture teaches that the final decision to accept or reject the revelation of God is in the hands of the sinner. Jesus warned that "unless you believe, you shall all likewise perish." This implies that while grace may bring the sinner to the threshold of redemption and prepare the heart to receive Christ, it is still the personal confession of the sinner that is necessary to seal the covenant of salvation. Even Luther confessed in his *Sermon on the Worthy Reception of the Sacrament* that church authorities should never force anyone to receive the Lord's Supper. After all, Luther reasoned, "the sacrament-even God himself- can bestow nothing on you against your will. Since God's gifts are so great, they demand a great hunger and desire, but they avoid and flee from a forced and unwilling heart" (*Luther's Works, Vol.42. ed. Martin O. Dietrich. Philadelphia: Fortress Press, 1949, p. 172*).

Those who propagate the "all of grace" position often resort to the statement made by Paul in which he said: "By the grace of God I am what I am: and his grace which was bestowed upon me was not found vain, but I labored more abundantly than they all: yet not I, but the grace of God which was with me." In this passage, however, Paul, self-titled "chief of sinners," attributes his blessings and successes to God. God forgave him, saved him, called him, and anointed him so that he was able to successfully evangelize the nations of Asia Minor. He gave the glory to God because in God he lived, and moved, and had his very being. Without God, there was nothing he could accomplish. Yet, he did not use the grace of God as an excuse to exempt himself from the need to "labor more abundantly than they all." He believed that much was required from him because much was given to him. And even though he accomplished much, the glory belongs to God because without the strength and grace of God, he would surely fail.

Therefore, while we rightly attribute our gains and successes to the grace of God, we must be careful not to send the wrong message to the world for who Christ died. When we say Christ died for the elect but not *all* are elect or not all can respond, I believe we are sending a wrong message to the world. Consider for a moment this situation: An evangelist goes into a stadium and preaches the gospel of Christ to thousands of people, mainly sinners. Before his call for a decision, he says, "By the way, not every one of you will be saved. Some of you are elected to destruction. But take heart. Since God always does what is right and what will bring glory to His name, you can be sure that if you are elected to destruction, which by the way means you need not come to this altar, though you will go to hell, be happy, for while you scream forever in hell, you can take heart in the fact that God is glorified. As for those of you who are elected to salvation, come. In fact, don't bother to come. You cannot come or else there will be human co-operation, which means it is not all of grace. Instead, right where you are, just believe in your heart Christ died for you, and confess with your mouth the Lord Jesus, and you will be saved. Sorry! You can't do that because there will be human cooperation, which will deny total grace." Twist and turn it however you like, this is what election boils down to, and it is neither the spirit nor the letter of the Bible. The Bible teaches that Christ died for the world. For this reason, He commanded His disciples to preach the gospel to all nations. Those who respond to His offer of grace will be saved. Those who reject it will perish. He stands at the door and knocks. Grace will keep Him waiting and knocking. But only you and I can make that final decision as to whether we will open the door and let Him in. In this sense, grace needs our help to help us.

A final thought to ponder. To those who think that my analogy and conclusion border on Pelagianism, consider this: When you as a Christian do something sinful or wrong, who is responsible? Who is to be blamed? You will agree that you are responsible for your wrongs. But if you do something good, who gets the credit? God does. We have established that fact. So, when we do good, grace gets the credit. But when we do wrong, we take the blame. Where is the logic in this? And why is it false to think that human cooperation extinguishes grace? Why is it morally abhorrent to deny humans the freedom of choice when choosing or not choosing Christ? And how is a decision for Christ different from any other choice we make during our daily lives? What force prompted me to buy apples rather than oranges this past week? Is grace operative in only certain aspects of my life and absent in others? We can go on, but in the end, we must confess that there is a paradox in grace, and though grace may knock at the door of our hearts, we are the only ones with the key to the door. The multitudes of people who have heard the gospel and have refused the invitation to salvation or have accepted it only to turn away later submit evidence not for election but free will, for the power to choose or reject. God has set before us life and death and desires that we choose life. He would not be giving us a choice if we had no choice in the matter.

Another verse of scripture used to void human response to the divine offer is that where Jesus said, you can do nothing without me. Is this statement to be taken literally? If it is taken literally then the conclusion is inescapable. Both the good and the bad that I do are empowered by Christ. And if Christ empowers the bad then I am not responsible for my wrongs. Clearly then this verse means something else. It means more likely that whatever we do, unless it is done for the glory of God, will amount to nothing with regards to divine recompense. Our lives may be full of sound and fury, but like Shakespeare's "poor player" who struts and frets his hour on the stage, at the judgment, it will be a tale told by an idiot, signifying nothing.

Once again, to say that God elects some to salvation and quickens them so that they might respond to Him, while He withholds grace from others, electing them to destruction, is a blasphemous attack on the God of love. I have two children, and I love them dearly. There is not a thing in my power that I would not do to make them happy. I am sure that all my readers feel the same way. Yet, who are we? We are sinners, evil men, and women. Why should we suppose that our love for our children could surpass the love of God, who is the embodiment of love? Jesus asked, "If you, being evil, know how to give good gifts to your children, how much more would not your Heavenly Father give the Holy Spirit to them that ask Him?" To say God has elected some to destruction is saying that we as sinful humans are more compassionate, loving, and merciful than God because none of us would condemn any of our children, regardless of wayward they might have become, to a life of misery and unhappiness. Such a charge against God cannot stand. Further, it should be noted that God has a vested interest in human creation. In Cur Deus Homo, Anselm of Canterbury suggested that one of the reasons God became man was because He was not going to allow His handiwork to be destroyed by sin. Humans were made in His image. God had something of Himself deposited in them. How then could He elect some of them to death? Instead, the case can be made that God does all that in His power to bring us to saving knowledge and experience. He took it upon Himself to send His Son to die for us. He sent His Holy Spirit to reveal Christ to us. But He could go no further without infringing upon the free will of humans –freedom which He invested in them and which He respects, but which He wills should be used to serve Him in love. When we take that simple step toward His already extended offer of salvation, like the returning prodigal son, we will discover that He was already on His way to embrace us and reconcile us to Himself, for He knows that we have chosen Him out of love and not out of coercion. In this way, the devil is hindered from accusing Him of acting on our behalf against our will.

So, under the influence of grace, Ruth approached Boaz as he slept, in the quiet of the night, and away from the eyes of others (3: 9). She was shocked to learn of his related interest in her from the day he first set sights on her. So too, those who seek divine favor will be surprised to discover that Jesus had His eyes on you while you toiled and that He was covertly pursuing you, waiting for you to invite Him into your heart and life. Even though you are the apple of His eyes, and although He wants you to be a part of His bride, He will never enforce His will on you. Instead, you must call on Him based on the completed work on Calvary's cross. You must step out in faith and respond to the offer of salvation. As you approach Him, you will be surprised how quickly He will reciprocate your affections.

Lesson 12: Ruth reminds us that we are under constant surveillance, whether we are aware of it.

Boaz said to her, "inasmuch as you did not follow young men, whether rich or poor, and now, my daughter, fear not; I will do for you all that you require: for all the people of my city know that you are a virtuous woman" (3: 10, 11). Observe, Boaz claimed that "all the people" knew Ruth to be a virtuous woman. On this, W.M. Smith commented: "Men and women are judged at their true worth even in this world, and even the wicked respect the upright and just. Of Nehemiah, it was reported to the king that "there is a man in thy kingdom in whose heart is the fear of the holy God."

There are more eyes on the saint than she would care to imagine. While a great cloud of witnesses cheers us on, many devils seek to eliminate us from the race. How important then is the warning to order our conversation aright and to live in obedience to the word of God. Jesus was fully aware that He was under observation, but He lived so pleasing to God He could boast, "the prince of this world comes and has nothing in me." Now He challenges believers to let their lights shine before men, so that their good works might be recognized, and that God might be glorified. And Paul cautions the saints to godliness, reminding them that they are epistles, read and known of all men. All eyes are upon us, including that of the Theos. He sees what no other person can. He sees the heart. He saw virtuous Mary among the women of Nazareth and chose her for His noble designs. He saw righteous Noah and saved him from the great deluge while the world perished. He saw righteous Lot and delivered him from the ill-fated Sodom. He saw the upright Job and boasted of his integrity among the sons of men. He saw the faith of Abraham and provided a lamb for a sacrifice. He saw the sorrow of Jabez and granted him his request for spiritual and material enlargement. All things are naked and open to Him. And when we stand at the Judgment Seat of Christ, we will be surprised to discover what He knew and what He saw, for the fire will manifest all things, whether they be good or bad. We are being monitored. Every idle word we speak is being recorded in the annals of judgment. Every cup of cold water we give to someone is also noted in the reward books. Therefore, let us put off the evil works of darkness and put on the new creation that is made after Christ.

Lesson 13: Ruth, in being blessed by Boaz, reminds us that benediction is both necessary and efficacious.

Boaz blessed her, saying, "The Lord bless you, my daughter." The benediction or "blessing" is neither a concoction of the Church nor the presumption of any individual. The Lord commanded it to His under-shepherds as a conduit of His graceful benevolence to His children. God issued the paradigm benediction as an example: "And the Lord spoke unto Moses, saying, Speak unto Aaron and unto his sons, saying, on this wise you shall bless the children of Israel, saying unto them, The Lord bless you, and keep you: The Lord make his face shine upon you, and be gracious unto you: The Lord lift up his countenance upon you and give you peace. And they shall put my name upon the children of Israel, and I will bless them" (Nu.6:22-27). In compliance, "Aaron lifted up his hand toward the people, and blessed them" (Leviticus 9:22). And others followed suit. Joshua blessed them and sent them away: and they went to their tents" (Joshua 22:6). And David, as soon as he "had finished offering burnt offerings and peace offerings, he blessed the people in the name of the LORD of hosts" (2Samuel 6:18). Likewise, "when

Solomon had finished praying all this prayer and supplication to the LORD, he arose from before the altar of the LORD, from kneeling on his knees with his hands spread up to heaven, and he stood, and blessed all the congregation of Israel with a loud voice" (1Kings 8:54-56). Under the Old covenant, however, the "blessing" was restricted to those of the Aaronic priesthood, and to the children of Israel. But as Grace subsumed the Law, so too Aaron's priesthood graciously stepped aside and gave way to that of a greater High Priest; One who was able to sympathize; One that bore gently with the ignorant; One who God called; One who was perfected through obedience; One who saves the obedient. And with the arrival of that great High Priest, who has passed through the heavens, Jesus the Son of God, the "blessing" was extended to include all people, even as Christ offered His own blood as a sacrifice for all. Christ blessed His disciples and the children brought to Him and authorized His under-shepherds to continue in like manner. Consequently, we observe a continual and bountiful supply of apostolic benedictions on all saints "scattered everywhere." The apostle Paul blessed the saints at Corinth: "The grace of the Lord Jesus Christ, and the love of God, and the communion of the Holy Spirit be with you all. Amen" (2 Corinthians 13:14). Jude blessed those sanctified and preserved: "Now to Him who can keep you from falling and present you faultless before the presence of his glory with exceeding joy. To God, the only wise, our Savior, be glory and majesty, dominion, and power, both now and ever. Amen" (Jude 1:24, 25). An unnamed writer blessed the tried and severely tempted Hebrew saints: "Now the God of peace, that brought again from the dead our Lord Jesus, that great shepherd of the sheep, through the blood of the everlasting covenant, Make you perfect in every good work to do his will, working in you that which is well-pleasing in his sight, through Jesus Christ; to whom be glory forever and ever. Amen" (Hebrews 13:20). And Peter blessed the scattered "strangers": "But the God of all grace, who has called us to his eternal glory by Christ Jesus, after you have suffered a while, make you perfect, establish, strengthen, settle you. To him be glory and dominion forever and ever. Amen" (1 Peter 5: 10, 11).

The Benediction is a powerful tool given to the Church for its edification, exhortation, and comfort, and its pronouncement signals the release of the said blessing. It must, however, proceed from a benevolent heart that desires to bestow a blessing and must be in accordance with the will of God. Otherwise, it is a mockery, futile and meaningless. With these admonitions in mind, let us then who are priests of the New Covenant, use the power of the "blessing" to bless and strengthen the weak, edify and establish the Church, settle differences, and make peace among us. We may not have "silver and gold" to give to anyone, but we do have the authority to release the blessings of the Lord to them. Therefore, as Boaz blessed Ruth, let us who are priests unto God continue to lift our hands towards the people and bless them with the blessings of the Lord.

Lesson 14: Ruth affirms the need for patience to allow the perfect unfolding of the divine will and purpose for our lives.

When Naomi heard of the events that transpired between Boaz and Ruth, how he had spread his covering over her and showered her with gifts and the promise of marriage, she advised Ruth, "Sit still, my daughter, until you know how the matter will fall" (3:18). Under the circumstances, that admonition was highly unusual. Here is a family who, just days earlier, returned home widowed, bankrupted, hopeless, and unable to redeem their inheritance, and now, only a few days later, stood on the threshold of greatness - redemption, restoration, and exaltation. Arguably, it would have been, for most people, the perfect occasion for spontaneous celebration, unrestrained emotions, and irrepressible joy. But the more mature Naomi was quite aware that such moments were not ideal for coherent thinking, logical choices, and intelligent decisions. If she intended to maximize this opportunity and capture the true essence and significance of the subject matter before her, she must allow the excitement to subside and give the powers of mind and spirit time to refocus. She knew from experience that the potential for disaster is greatest when "anyone thinks he stands," and wisely cautioned Ruth to "sit still." Alas! How many potential gains are squandered, how many signal victories forfeited, how many promotions are denied, how many blessings redirected, how many opportunities lost, simply because we could not "sit still until we know how the matter falls."

The wise man said there is a time for everything. There is a time to be on the potter's wheel and in motion to facilitate the hands of Providence in unfolding His grand design and purpose for our lives, and a time to "be still" in His presence. For stillness is essential to the reception of Divine interposition. Moses said unto the children of Israel, as they stood on the banks of the Red Sea, hemmed in on all sides by certain death, "Stand still, and see the salvation of the Lord." Stillness is also essential to the reception of Divine instruction. Again, Moses said unto the children of Israel, "Stand still, and I will hear what the Lord will command concerning you" (Nu.9: 8). Stillness is also essential to the reception of Divine assurance. When Mary was informed that she was divinely favored to bear the holy Child, the Scripture notes she "pondered these things in her heart." She could not comprehend how conception was possible without the aid of a man. And how will she explain her condition when signs of pregnancy become visible? Will Joseph believe her story? Will her friends, family, and neighbors believe a fantastical tale of "immaculate conception" by some Holy Ghost, considering she was already engaged? Her dilemma was understandable, and she knew any attempt to defend, explain or justify her situation would have been futile and foolish. So she resigned herself to the will of the Almighty and said, "Be it unto me according to Thy Word." In the end, God vindicated her faith and rewarded her bountifully. Today she is not despised but instead revered by millions. He does all things well.

Maybe you, dear reader, are caught in circumstances inexplicable. You have no idea how you arrived at where you are and are equally clueless about how to get out. And as you struggle, taking matters into your own hands, the situation appears to worsen. You seem stuck in a dilemma, sinking further with every attempt at self-redemption. Indeed, the temptation to struggle is intense, induced by many conflicting philosophies that vie for the right of application. But you must deny them that right on the ground that God will not suffer you to be tempted above that which you are able, but will, with the temptation, make a way of escape that is bearable. It matters not how fierce the opposition may appear; you have nothing to fear, for "He makes wars to cease unto the end of the earth; he breaks the bow and cuts the spear in sunder; he burns the chariot in the fire. Be still and know that I am God: I will be exalted among the heathen and exalted in the earth" (Psalms 46: 8-10). Sit still, therefore, and allow God to show you the way out. And let patience do her perfect work, that you may be perfect and entire, wanting nothing (James 1:4).

Lesson 15: The divine dealing with Ruth is a pointed reminder that God is at work in every person's life to incorporate them into the plan of the ages and bring them to His Son Jesus, in whom they will find true and lasting happiness.

Fate, it would appear, had dealt an unfair hand to Ruth. She was given a sickly husband, who could not provide her a house or children to call her own, and who did not provide for her future. He had left her alone and dependent on others for moral, spiritual, and financial support at his passing. As all women did, she had hoped that marriage would be for better and not for worse. Unfortunately for her, it seemed as though it was for worse. And if not for the existence of a caring God and the working of Divine providence to make "all things work together for good to them that love the Lord," her situation would have been worse. But through it all, a Sovereign, Omniscient God was at work, orchestrating events, good and adverse, to guide and direct her path to the heavenly Boaz. Sure, she lost her husband, but her marriage into the family of Elimelech was not altogether a loss. Through it, she was brought into a precious union with Naomi, her mother-in-law, and eventually into the perfect marriage with Boaz.

As Dr. Leggett pointed out, God worked His purposes of salvation in history in the ordinary lives of people like Ruth and Naomi, living in very adverse circumstances. But there are no ordinary lives, and the genealogy points out that something far more has been happening in these seemingly insignificant events in Moab. This simple story, he notes, opens like a stream into a greater river of hope that includes the whole world. Therefore, never think that what you do in obedience to God during your setbacks is insignificant. Little acts of faithfulness under adverse circumstances can become eternally significant.

Likely, some of you who read these words find yourselves in a similar position as the once bereaved Ruth. Fate, it appears, has dealt you an unfair hand. Perhaps your life partner has been taken away from you in the prime of their life, leaving you lonely, defenseless, and dependent. Maybe you feel cheated and wronged, and as a result, you have become bitter and unforgiving, indifferent to the suffering of others, and angry at the success of others. Once not enough for your hectic schedule, your days are now much too long, and you sometimes wish that the night will never end. A vibrant life has been slowed to a mechanical existence. When in the company of others, you sport a veneer that says all is well and you are in control, but under the mask, you are hurting deeply. Even the feeble attempt at revival is smothered by the notion that it is too late to start afresh. You wish it were just a bad dream that would come quickly to an end. Still, some of you may have suffered other forms of losses. Maybe it is the loss of a dream, the wreck of a marriage and home through divorce or infidelity, or the loss of filial love, and because of it, your life has come to a terminus. You feel you have had your chance at happiness and must now give way to others. You feel reduced, inferior, a destined loser. But there is one thing you must know: As far as God is concerned, your life journey is not yet over. That this booklet has found its way into your hands is indisputable evidence that Divine providence is still at work in your life to make you into "the vessel that seems fit unto Him." You have a High priest who has been "touched with the feelings of your infirmities," having been tempted in such manner Himself, and who, now triumphantly exalted at the right hand of God, lives evermore to make intercession for you. He has his eyes set on you with the desire of drawing you to Himself and has allowed the circumstances in your life to bring you in the proximity of His grace and love. Now you must go boldly to Him, on the ground that He died for your sins and rose again for your justification and let Him cover you with the garment of salvation. He will not reject you but will receive you with a pledge of eternal love and care. In Him, and with Him, your life will begin anew, even as one "born again." He will rebuild your shattered dreams and help you to have them fulfilled. He will be a husband to you and a friend that sticks closer than a brother. You will know true joy, peace, love and happiness, and life more abundantly. The reproach and disappointments of the past will fade harmlessly into distant memory as "old things are passed away, and all things have become new." But you must be bold in your approach. You must be determined to overcome the obstacles in the path to your Boaz. Indeed, the virtuous Ruth hesitated when Naomi prompted her advance to Boaz. Suppose he rejects me for my looks. Suppose he thinks little of me for my presumption. Suppose he disdains me for my different racial and cultural heritage [The post-exilic prophets Ezra and Nehemiah had threatened any union between Jews and non-Jews]. Suppose I jeopardize his future and social standing. Such questions must have raced through her mind. And no doubt, as you think of approaching Jesus, many such thoughts will distract and discourage you. But you must penetrate the obstacles and press your case for redemption. Christ died for all. You are not a traitor to your religious tradition if you choose him as Savior. Press your case despite the traditions of men. God is on your side. You have no reason to fear what man can do to you.

Boaz awoke in the middle of the night and was fearfully but wonderfully surprised to find the secret desire of his heart lying at his feet, seeking his approval and espousal. He responded immediately, "Blessed are you of the Lord, my daughter: for you have shown more kindness in the latter end than at the beginning because you did not follow after younger men, whether rich or poor. And now, my daughter, fear not; I will do for you all that you required" (3:10, 11). In these words, Boaz intimates a prolonged interest in Ruth. After all, how else could he have known that she followed not after the young and restless rich men of her generation? However, the tone of his response infers that, as far as he was concerned, he never stood a chance of winning the affections of this fair maiden. He was much more advanced in years than Ruth. And for another, wealth, it appears, was not a deciding factor since there were also other wealthy young men in contention. Hence the surprise at her marriage proposal, and the spontaneous response to her request, are understandable.

Even so, Jesus, the heavenly Boaz, patiently waits and watches over us as we glean the fields of life, desiring us, dreaming of making us exclusively His. But alas! The attractions of this world, the pleasures of sin, and the desires of youth have wooed many of us away from

Him. We hasten after the fleeting things of this world - the lust of the flesh, the lust of the eyes, and the pride of life. Boaz is too old-fashioned for our modern world, we say. Did not even your prophet say there is no beauty in Him that we should desire Him? But see from Boaz how Jesus loves you and how readily He will take you to be His bride. He will redeem you and recover your inheritance. He will remain faithful to you all the days of your life. You will share with him the riches of his glory and never again know the sorrows of Moab. So go ahead, stake your claim on the Lord Jesus Christ even as Ruth staked her claim on Boaz, and you will be surprised how readily he will respond to your plea for redemption, "even in the morrow," will He attend to this matter.

As Boaz received Ruth, the heavenly Boaz will joyously receive you, and like Ruth, your life too will be transformed overnight. She was childless for the ten years she sojourned in Moab (1:4-5), and now, in a few short weeks in Bethlehem, she was blessed beyond expectation. In twenty-two short verses, she moved from rags to riches, and the fulcrum of that swing was none other than Boaz. He made a difference in her life. The story concludes with a happy end: "So Boaz took Ruth, and she was his wife" (4:13). Those who come to Christ and make Him their bridegroom will write a story with a similar end. They will discover that Love Conquers All.

Hagar
Mama, Don't Cry
Texts: Gen 16; 21:9-17; 25:12; Gal 4:24,25

Text 1: The Beginning:

Genesis 16:1-16:

Now Sarai, Abram's wife, had borne him no children. And she had
an Egyptian maidservant whose name was Hagar. So Sarai said to
Abram, "See now, the Lord has restrained me from bearing children.
Please, go into my maid; perhaps I shall obtain children by her." And
Abram heeded the voice of Sarai. Then Sarai, Abram's wife, took
Hagar, her maid, the Egyptian, and gave her to her husband Abram
to be his wife after Abram had dwelt ten years in the land of Canaan.
So he went into Hagar, and she conceived. And when she saw that
she had conceived, her mistress became despised in her eyes.
Then Sarai said to Abram, "My wrong be upon you! I gave my maid
into your embrace, and when she saw that she had conceived, I
became despised in her eyes. The Lord judge between you and me."
So Abram said to Sarai, "Indeed your maid is in your hand; do to her
as you please." And when Sarai dealt harshly with her, she fled from
her presence.
Now the Angel of the Lord found her by a spring of water in the
wilderness, by the spring on the way to Shur. And He said, "Hagar,
Sarai's maid, where have you come from, and where are you
going?"
She said, "I am fleeing from the presence of my mistress Sarai."
The Angel of the Lord said to her, "Return to your mistress, and
submit yourself under her hand." Then the Angel of the Lord said to
her, "I will multiply your descendants exceedingly so that they shall
not be counted for multitude." And the Angel of the Lord said to her:
"Behold, you are with child,
And you shall bear a son.
You shall call his name Ishmael,
Because the Lord has heard your affliction.
He shall be a wild man;
His hand shall be against every man,
And every man's hand against him.

And he shall dwell in the presence of all his brethren."
Then she called the name of the Lord who spoke to her, You-Are-the-God-Who-Sees; for she said, "Have I also here seen Him who sees me?" Therefore, the well was called Beer Lahai Roi; it is between Kadesh and Bered.
So Hagar bore Abram a son; and Abram named his son, whom Hagar bore, Ishmael. Abram was eighty-six years old when Hagar bore Ishmael to Abram.

Text 2: Sixteen years later:

Genesis 21:9-17: And Sarah saw the son of Hagar the Egyptian, which she had borne to Abraham, mocking. Wherefore she said to Abraham, Cast out this bondwoman and her son: for the son of this bondwoman shall not be heir with my son, even with Isaac. And the thing was very grievous in Abraham's sight because of his son. And God said to Abraham, Let it not be grievous in thy sight because of the lad, and because of thy bondwoman; in all that Sarah hath said to thee, hearken to her voice; for in Isaac shall thy seed be called. And also of the son of the bondwoman will I make a nation, because he is thy seed. And Abraham rose early in the morning, took bread, and a skin of water, and gave it to Hagar, put it on her shoulder, and the child, and sent her away: and she departed, and wandered in the wilderness of Beersheba. And the water was spent in the skin, and she cast the child under one of the shrubs. And she went and sat her down apart from him a good way off, as it were a bowshot: for she said, Let me not see the child's death. And she sat apart from him, raised her voice, and wept. And God heard the lad's voice; and the angel of God called to Hagar out of heaven, and said to her, What ails you, Hagar? Fear not, for God hath heard the lad's voice where he is.

Text 3: The symbolic meaning:

Galatians 4:22-27: For it is written that Abraham had two sons: the one by a bondwoman, the other by a freewoman. But he who was of the bondwoman was born according to the flesh, and he of the freewoman through promise, which things are symbolic. For these are the two covenants: the one from Mount Sinai which gives birth to bondage, which is Hagar— for this Hagar is Mount Sinai in Arabia and corresponds to Jerusalem which now is and is in bondage with her children— 26 but the Jerusalem above is free, which is the mother of us all. For it is written:

"Rejoice, O barren, you who do not bear! Break forth and shout, you who are not in labor! The desolate has many more children than she who has a husband."

***

Who is Hagar? Apart from the fact that her Egyptian name resembles the root of the Arabic which means "flight," and that it was a fitting adaptation to the circumstances of her life, we know nothing or her genealogy other than what legend supplies. Fable has it that she was an Egyptian princess, a daughter of the same Pharaoh who sought to add Sarah to his possessions, who chose to proselyte with Abraham and his wife when they departed Egypt for their former homeland. This legend goes on to say that she became so attached to Sarah when she told her father of her desire to emigrate, the king was furious and asked if she knew she would be a handmaid, to which she replied that it was better to be a handmaid in the tents of Abraham than to be a princess in an Egyptian palace. However, such unsubstantiated contributions must be dismissed either as an attempt to minimize the atrocity of slavery or as a platform to magnify the virtues of one religious experience over another. While the latter assumption is not inconceivable or unlawful, one must question why an Egyptian princess would trade her liberty and regal privilege for that of a handmaiden when the famous Hammurabi's Code was clear on the expectations of such a role:

> If she has given a maid to her husband and she has borne children and afterward that maid has made herself equal with her mistress, because she has borne children her mistress shall not sell her for money, she shall reduce her to bondage and count her among female slaves.

Not only were there serious consequences for attempting to be a human being equal in the sight of God to all others, but the whole experience of surrogate motherhood was humiliating to say the least. If a handmaiden was chosen for surrogacy, she was required to have intercourse upon the stomach of the barren wife with her face veiled, while the husband was supposed to see the face of his wife and imagine it to be his wife, and the wife would ensure that neither husband nor handmaiden derives any pleasure from this experience. Then nine months later, when the child was ready to be delivered, the pregnant handmaid must bear the baby on the knees of the barren wife, and the midwife must hand over the newborn baby to its new mother as the distraught handmaid looked on tearfully with a broken heart.

Suffice it to say, however, the Bible seeks no contribution from men to aid its completeness, and the essential truth about Hagar, as given in that revelation, must be grasped from the fragments of truth therein. What does the Biblical record have to say about Hagar? Was she real or allegorical? What are we to learn from her life, sufferings, and her ultimate triumph? These issues form the heart of this booklet.

&

Hagar is first presented to us as an Egyptian slave girl who had very little say in her future. How she became a slave no one knows. Maybe she was sold in the discharge of family debts. Maybe she was just snatched by slave traders. But what is known is that Abraham purchased her from a slave trader in Egypt and brought her into his home as the handmaiden of Sarah, his wife. Even back then it seems like the clergy, of whom Abraham represented the "father of faith," validated slave- trading and even participated in it themselves. Sarah, on the other hand, was barren and her condition was a cause of concern for the family especially since God had promised Abraham a "seed through which all the nations of the world will be blessed." But how will this seed come into the world if she could not conceive? Perhaps she was overcome with guilt that she was singularly responsible for frustrating the promise of God and for denying the world of its greatest blessing. That feeling would certainly explain her hastiness in advancing a remedy for the problem. Clearly, she felt the onus was on her to resolve this dilemma. She did not give providence a chance to honor its promises but allowed faith and trust to be trampled to death by human logic and reason. Perhaps she thought God expected her to use common sense to make it all happen, after all, it was easy to reason that since the promise was made to Abraham, the nature of the child's mother was not of dire significance. This kind of reasoning would surely explain her hastiness in recommending the handmaiden as a surrogate mother. Abraham fell prey to her suggestion and the ceremony took place. He did not appear to object in any way or form but allowed his own inner desperation for greatness to blind his sense of good judgment. The flesh can drive those who are full of faith can be driven by the flesh when the reward is self-aggrandizement. The handmaid became pregnant and bore Abraham his firstborn son, Ishmael, which means, "God hears." Thus, Hagar became the foundress of the Ishmaelites and Arab peoples from whom Mohammed, the founder of Islam, is deemed to have had his roots. After the birth of Ishmael, she underwent an almost instantaneous character transformation, no longer servile and submissive, but proud and arrogant, juxtaposing for the position as the lead actress in the household of Abraham. She used motherhood to despise the childless Sarah and taunted her relentlessly, and in return the jealous and infuriated freewoman sent her packing to the wilderness.

Indeed, the sixteenth chapter of Genesis, in the words of Herbert Lockyer, is "like the shortest verse in the Bible ... saturated with tears." Clearly there is folly in all the parties involved. Sarah, a child of faith, should have known that God was able to raise up children to Abraham, even if He had to make them from stones. In the end, she rightly confessed, "My wrong," but not before her sin bore bitter fruit, and not before she commenced a war that has separated nations through the ages and soaked the earth with precious human blood.

Equally so, the "father" of faith ought to have known that God does not resort to unjust and immoral means to justify His ends and should have refused the suggestion to take his handmaid. He should have obeyed the law of God but instead he "harkened to her voice," and like Adam, became a co-conspirator in the crime. It was fitting then that after Hagar became pregnant and obnoxious, Sarah blamed Abraham, saying, "My wrong be upon thee: the Lord judge between me and thee" (Ge.16:5). And she was right! Blame, regardless of how justifiable it may appear, never transfers guilt or punishment. Abraham was the head of his household, and the decision was his to make. He knew Sarah was the flesh of his flesh and bone of his bone, and when they were joined in holy matrimony they became, in the eyes of God, as one flesh. Their plan for securing an heir was in essence polygamy, and polygamy has always been in violation of the Creator's plan for marriage (Gen.2:24). They had both lived long enough and experienced life sufficiently to know that more than one partner interferes with the mathematics of a marriage union. For it is two that becomes one, not three!

The handmaiden, on the other hand, may not have had much say in her role especially if she was purchased in the slave market, but still, she should not have participated in this unholy alliance. The worse that could have resulted from a refusal to bear her master a child was to be reduced to a female slave in his harem or to be driven from the home. In either case, she would have retained her integrity and womanhood. Hence, regardless of the angle from which this drama is viewed, all parties involved were guilty of a lack of faith and trust in God. Those of the household of faith were guilty of the greater sin because they had more light, and to whom much is given, much is required.

The universal lesson that should be indelibly inked with tears upon our hearts is that any attempt to secure the promise of God by means that are not prescribed or sanctioned by God will produce heartbreak and pain. The fates of these three individuals should serve as a monument of discouragement to all those who are tempted to use any aids of human concocting for the attainment of personal ends, even if those means appear legitimate and justifiable, and even if the cultural standards make them lawful and acceptable. All such devices will lead to sorrows of the heart. God is faithful and is well able to perform all that He has promised. If He promised a child, He would deliver that child though child-bearing years may pass and though the reproductive capacities might long be dead. He does all things in the fullness of His time and for the glory of His name. We need only, like Joshua and Caleb, to "wholly" trust in Him, and in the end, we will obtain a good report through faith.

Hagar, often considered a victim in this saga, and the one most worthy of our sympathy is not totally without blame for the judgment she received from Sarah. Upon discovering her pregnancy she became altogether a different person, no longer meek and subservient, but the haughty carrier of Abraham's child. She was fertile and Sarah was barren. She will bear children for Abraham while Sarah cannot. She will be a mother and Sarah a foster parent. Likely, she refused to perform the regular, menial, daily chores of a handmaiden and to pay the usual respect to her mistress. Yet in her reaction to Sarah after her pregnancy, one cannot help but notice the temptations incident to a new position, especially when that role is thrust upon the immature of heart and experience. Her reaction, though childish and immature, was not unexpected under such circumstances. She simply could not handle her blessing and in the end, it became her curse.

Interestingly, some commentators castigate Abraham, not for a lack of faith to believe God was able to give him the promised child, but for poor judgment in choosing Hagar, a person of lower class and bearing, to be involved in this higher program of God. For example, *The Homiletic Commentary (p.238)* uses this platform to address the issue of the evils of abolishing social distinctions. The argument is as follows:

Those who are suddenly raised in the social scale are tempted to pride and insolence and will reproach those who are the means of their advancement because they are not fitted by natural endowment and training for the higher stations in life. The argument goes on to say that human experience has proved that, in many cases, the morals of men have been entirely changed by their sudden exaltation to place, power, or wealth. They become full of conceit, scornful and reproachful to others, even to their benefactors. In this case, Hagar is deemed to have mistaken the grounds of the favors bestowed upon her, falling prey to the same "delusion" as those who have been advanced from humble stations by the artificial regenerators of society, men who only cared to serve their selfish ends, and who have regarded the poor and lowly as steps along which they might climb to power and importance.

This argument clearly advocates the propagation of a caste system among peoples and the strict maintenance of those classes for the social structure to function. It leaves no room for the advancement or development of individuals. It is fatalistic in approach. Man must adhere to the ant-colony mentality. If you were born a worker ant you must die a worker ant. If you are a soldier ant, you must remain a soldier ant for the rest of your existence. And if you are a "stink" ant, you must remain a stinker the rest of your life. The question that begs an answer is, who is fitted by natural endowment and training for the higher stations of life? What makes a man or woman fit for such roles? Is it the color of his skin, the manner of his speech, or his table etiquette? And what natural endowment does the "higher" class possess over the lower? Are they in possession of a superior intellect? Did Abraham display superior wisdom when he dabbled in the slave market and when he passively consented to Sarah's plan? Did he act like a man of a higher station when he booted his wife and adolescent child into the desert knowing they would die? And what about Hagar, was she delusional to believe she could become a better person? Are all those who desire to better themselves delusional? Is the desire for excellence only a mirage? How then do we explain all the rags to riches stories we love to tell? I guess the answer would be that those individuals were born to a higher station, and it was their destiny to succeed. If such is the case, then how will men know their destiny unless they strive for excellence? As for the argument that the morals of some men quickly degenerate when promoted, the same can be said of some men within the same social class. Are we to say that there is no effect on the morals of people within one social order when there are changes within that structure? To believe this is so is to be truly delusional. Every class of society has people who are full of conceit, scornful, and reproachful to others, even those who assisted in their success. And one does not have to be raised from one social scale to another to become bloated with pride and insolence. Those behaviors are common within every social class. In fact, pride and insolence have little to do with social rank or elevation. Some of the poorest have the purest spirit and some of the most privileged are unbearably snobbish and disdainful, egotistical, and pompous.

Second, those who have taken part in the abolishing of social distinctions are the first to complain of the evils caused thereby. They, like Sarah, complain of their troubles to excuse themselves and often make rash appeals to divine justice - "The Lord judge between me and thee." Here again, the commentary seems to be more of a judgment on those "artificial regenerators" of society. If you abolish social distinctions, you will pay the price. If you make the fatal mistake of trying to educate, acculturate, elevate, or nurture those of a lower class, you will be the first to complain and seek divine aid. The tone of the commentary seems to make a subtle reference to the emancipation of slaves. But who made slaves. Men did! Therefore it is man who created that class. And it is men who have created classes to maintain their perceived distinctiveness. The rich, the intelligent, the noble of birth, all flock together and create clubs, societies, orders, associations, and organizations to secure their "uniqueness" and to insulate themselves from dissimilar creatures. In so doing they also insulate themselves from the rich diversity of cultures and experiences that add spice and color to otherwise monochromatic lives.

The argument advanced for the maintenance of social classes is that the recognition of original rights must be enforced. Therefore, authority to deal with Hagar must be returned to Sarah - "Do to her as it pleases thee." But to return Hagar to her mistress was certainly not the best way to recognize original rights. To truly recognize original rights Abraham should have freed the woman. What she chose to do with that freedom was hers to decide. Many proslavery proponents have argued that the economic and mental state of the slave is far better than most people. This is not an issue for them to decide and this is certainly no justifiable reason for holding people against their will. Who determines what factors precipitate economic and emotional well-being? One man's meat is another man's poison. Some retreat to the mountains for solace, and some favor a life of quiet contemplation. Some prefer a simple, nomadic life. Some pursue wealth, some women, some fame and fortune, every man to his own order. But perhaps it is because so many trample the road to material prosperity thinking it is the answer to man's quest for fulfillment that Jesus deemed it necessary to slam the material-minded, saying, "A man's life consists not in the abundance of things which he possesses...For what profits a man if he gains the whole world and loses his own soul. Or what shall a man give in exchange for his soul?"

The fourth argument for the maintenance of social distinctions is that the evils brought about by sudden and violent changes in the social state are never fully remedied. To extrapolate from this singular experience such a bold theory is both reckless and irresponsible. Were all violent changes in social states caused by a disruption in social distinctions? Does elevating others from lower economic classes cause all social upheavals? In all these arguments, Hagar is seen as a class of lesser human being who is illiterate, barbaric, unteachable, and without the capacity for development. She must be judged before being given a chance. She must remain a victim of her circumstances. Any investment in her development is a waste of resources for it would only be to the detriment of all parties and create irreparable damage to society.

God gives grace to the humble, and He exalts them in due time, but equally so, He also humbles those who exalt themselves. How appropriate then is the warning, "If any man thinks he stands, let him take heed lest he fall." Unfortunately for Hagar, conceiving a child for Abraham did not change her role as handmaiden nor did it lessen his love for his faithful and beloved wife. Besides, Sarah was not going to allow the pregnancy to interfere with the sanity of her mind and the sanctity of her home and marriage. Taunted to the point where it had become overbearing, she responded with righteous indignation and made life a daily, living hell for the precocious Hagar. Finally, unable to continue the battle she started, Hagar surrendered and fled for refuge in the desert. In her response, we cannot help but identify with the foolishness of hasty actions in times of trial and difficulty. Like her, we all react to adversities in a similar fashion when castigated. We sit in our wilderness of self-pity and gloom and try to figure a way out of our dilemma all by ourselves. Little are we prepared to accept our lot as ordained by God for our good and so we hurriedly attempt to change the circumstances of our lives. In the end, we find that unless we return from whence we came, retrace our steps, and conquer that which we have stumbled over, we will never be able to move onwards with a clear path behind us. This is why God commanded her to return to the house of Abraham.

Return and submit! Why, because closure is necessary to avoid a fragmented life. If a fracture is not looked after you will be left with a limp. It will slow you down and you will carry a pain throughout life. Life is a journey. It must be undertaken systematically and progressively. Stop and take as long as is necessary but fix the problem before you move on.

As she rested on a rock in the wilderness, confused and angry, blinded by tears, bemoaning her fate, holy angels appeared to her and commanded her to "return to your mistress, and submit yourself to her authority...[for] Behold, you are with child, and you shall bear a son; and you shall call his name Ishmael" (Ge.16: 1-11).

> The angel called Hagar by name, asks her questions, not for information, but to show God has an interest in her and to draw out an honest response from her. God's government over all His creatures is not a heartless routine but proceeds upon an exact knowledge of the condition and wants of each. One of the purposes of revelation is to teach us the personal interest which God takes in us. And that by imparting to us, not mysteries which are irrelevant, but to correct our sinful courses and teach us duty.

In response to that divinely commissioned visitation in the wilderness of Shur, Hagar cried out in hope, "You see me."

> God, said the Greeks, is All Eye. Not a feeble and changing glance but pure and perfect scrutiny. This thought may be one of grandeur but also one of terror. We are never safe from the never-closing eyes of God. It should also cause us to think of consolation in sorrow. He knows of our desire to be pure and good. Finally, it is

a thought that should give hope in danger. He sees to help and save.

How can we not be comforted by the care exercised over the lonely and the oppressed by the all-seeing God? She named the well where God spoke to her and revealed the future of her son, "Beth-lahairoi," meaning, "the well of Him that lives and sees me." That meant a lot to her, for, unlike the Egyptian gods who could not see even though they stared with unblinking eyes both night and day at the desert, this God of Abraham sees everything and acts on the behalf of the tired, the abused, the weary, and the worn. His eyes never cease to wander to and fro the ends of the earth beholding the works of the children of men. The great prophet Samuel, as he prepared to anoint Eliab as king of Israel, instead of David, learned that even the thoughts of the human heart are naked and open to His penetrating gaze, for "the Lord sees not as man sees." While man looks at the outward appearance, God looks at the heart. That day Hagar learned two important and complementary truths about God: He lives, and He sees. "To God's omnipotence there is nothing impossible; and to God's omniscience, there is nothing invisible" (Secker).

Ah, friend! Perhaps you are mistreated, abused, an outcast, downtrodden, and like Hagar, on the run, heading for you know not where. Presently God seems a million miles away from you, and indifferent to your situation and misfortune. A million thoughts race through your mind and none of them seem the right thing to do. Well, if you stop running, sit still, wipe your tears, and lift up your head, you will see Him standing before you and you will hear His comforting voice saying, I see your tears and I am with you always, even to the end of this age. So don't cry. Just obey my instructions and will end well. As God knew the anguish of her soul, so too He identifies with your suffering and feels your pain, for we have not a High Priest who cannot be touched with the feelings of our infirmities, but who was in all points tempted like as we are. And because of His identification with our infirmities and His victory over every trial and temptation that came His way, He is supremely qualified to deliver those in like temptation.

Contrary to her expectations God commanded her to return to Sarah and Abraham. Two wrongs do not make a right. It was a difficult thing to do, but whatever God commands to be done, divine grace supplies the energy to perform it. Undoubtedly, had she succumbed to self-loathing and persisted in remaining in the wilderness, she would have died. But despite the potential shame and embarrassment that awaited her, she returned home in obedience to the command of God. Dr. Alexander Whyte praises Hagar for her submission to the divine will. He writes:

> Hagar, by reason of the extremity of her sorrow; by reason of the utter desolateness and brokenness of her heart; and by reason of the sovereign grace and abounding mercy of God - Hagar, I say, stands out before us in the very foremost rank of faith, and trust, and experience, and assurance. Hagar, to me, stands out among God's very electest saints. Hagar has only one or two who can stand beside her in her discovery of God, in her nearness to God, in her face-to-face fellowship with God, in the instructiveness, in the comfort, and in the hopefulness of her so close communion with God...The best and most blessed of them all was not more or better blessed than was Hagar the polluted outcast on her weeping way to Shur. The pure in heart shall see God.

She obeyed God and received from Him the assurance that even though her son Ishmael will not be the promised heir, he will be great. And she understood for the first time, that she, like any other person in the world, in or out of the household of Israel, was an object of God's special love and providential care and that the promises of God, linked to obedience to His Word, can be appropriated by anyone with faith in God.

It is not without significance that the Biblical record mentions the "angel of the Lord found her by a well of water." Nor is this the first incident in the Bible where the expression, "the angel of the Lord," is employed in the Holy Writ. This expression is held by many scholars to refer to a pre-incarnation manifestation of Jesus, the Son of God. The message then is that the Angel of the Lord still finds us in our extremities, like Jonah, when we are running from our assigned duties, and like John Mark, when we try to evade the sufferings and shame of the cross that we are called to bear and bring us back to where we turned aside. So Hagar returned home to her mistress and bore the eighty-six years old Abraham their child, and they all dwelt together in the same house for the next fourteen years. When Abraham was one hundred years old, Isaac, the long-awaited child of promise was eventually born to him and Sarah. But the happiness ushered in by the new baby was short-lived. As the child grew, so did a sibling rivalry for affection. Ishmael was jealous because of the attention given to Isaac and all the talk about his special birthright. This in turn created discord between Abraham and Sarah. And so it was that the jealous feud, which began with the two mothers, now continued with the two sons. Ishmael's reaction to Isaac was genetic. Hagar did not learn submission. The son did not submit. Indeed it is that he that sow to the wind shall reap the whirlwind! This time, however, Sarah reacted more viciously than she did on the first occasion. She had watched as her husband cradled and loved the child of another woman for fourteen long years. For fourteen years she endured the pain, the mockery, and the teasing. For fourteen years she vexed her righteous soul with the unlawful acts of the bondwoman. And now, to add fuel to fire, her son was being teased and vexed by the son of the bondwoman. This was the straw that broke the camel's back. With irresistible wrath, she compelled Abraham to drive both Hagar and Ishmael into the wilderness and he complied. With tears streaming down his beard he watched the young son of his loins walk away into the setting sun, knowing fully well that unless there is divine intervention on their behalf, the boy and his mother would not survive the wilderness. Artists through the centuries have tried to depict this sad scene. The masterpiece painting, "Hagar in the Wilderness," shows the boy lying on his back, dying of thirst, with his mother praying that she might not see the death of her child. But her extremity became God's opportunity. Even though this time she might be faulted for having openly despised Sarah and Isaac, God was still full of tender mercy and sent angels to her rescue. The heavenly messengers asked, "What is the matter with you, Hagar? Do not fear, for God had heard the voice of the lad where he is." Then God opened her eyes and she saw a well of water, and she went and filled the skin with water, and gave the lad a drink. And God was with the lad (Ge.21: 14-20).

Although Hagar was the instigator of Sarah's fury on this occasion, the Lord still visited her, comforted her, and opened her eyes that she might see a well of water to revive the critically dehydrated Ishmael. Surely God is merciful and is still prepared to forgive transgressors "seventy times seven." The bottle she received from Abraham was empty, but God gave her a well that could not be exhausted, and her son was saved from the jaws of death. In the first visitation, the angel brought comfort but also demanded submission. In the second visitation, the angel brought water and gave Hagar the assurance that her son will be blessed and become prosperous. Ishmael grew up in the wilderness of Paran and gained fame as an archer. When Abraham died, he returned from exile to help Isaac with the burial (Gen.25: 9). As God had promised, he became the father of twelve princes (Gen.25: 16), as well as a daughter, Mahalath, who later married Esau, son of Isaac (Gen.28: 9). Ishmael died at the age of one hundred and thirty-seven (Gen.25: 17).

The last scene with Hagar may well be the saddest of all. She departs for Egypt, her homeland, to find Ishmael a wife (Ge.21:21). What is so sad is that her decision to return to Egypt, a type of the world of sin and idolatry, is proof that the religion demonstrated by Abraham and Sarah was not a goodly pearl worth desiring or pursuing. How could Abraham persuade anyone to his faith when he acquiesced to his wife's instigation of wrongdoing? How could he be a witness to grace when he stood by and allowed a woman carrying his child to be driven out into a dangerous and lonely wilderness, giving her a bottle of water for sustenance? And how could Hagar become a disciple of the faith of Abraham when he could not protect her and when his wife displayed nothing else but selfishness, arrogance, and cruelty? The truth is that Hagar's total "faith" experience was gleaned from her life with Abraham and Sarah. They were the ambassadors of the faith to her heathen heart. They were her epistles of virtuous living to her untrained mind. But how did they read? She obviously saw them as hypocrites because we are told she wanted to return to Egypt and to idolatry and worldliness. Hagar saw nothing worth emulating, nothing worth desiring, and nothing that glorified

God in the lives of her masters. As the redeemed of the Lord they had an obligation to let their "lights so shine before men" that they might see the good works and glorify God. They failed, and she lost faith.

> Abraham and Sarah were the Church. And the church has often been accused of persecuting men and women, under mistaken zeal, making them outcasts and wanderers. Yet, such action can never close the door on divine mercy and compassion (*Candlish*).

Before closing our discussion on Hagar there is one final lesson to consider. And that is, according to the apostle Paul, the story of Hagar is also an allegory to distinguish the working of Law from Grace (Gal.4:21-31). This allegorical meaning, however, must never be used to minimize the reality of what happened to the household of Abraham, nor must it be allowed to distract us from the spiritual lessons that we have learned. These were real people who made real common mistakes and who suffered dearly because of their errors. And their story is recorded in the Holy Writ for our example and admonition that we might avoid the path to filial heartbreak. Likewise, the God of Abraham was not allegorical but real, and so too was His love, mercy, compassion, provision, protection, and promise. The divine dealing with Hagar is poignant proof that God is rich in mercy and that He continues to reach out graciously to all men regardless of what they might have done to deserve their fate or to incur their present circumstances. With that in mind, let us return to the allegory presented to the Galatians who had begun their pilgrimage by faith but were tempted to return to the bewitching influence of the Law to obtain justification with God.

The Typical Meaning

Hagar is the bondwoman and therefore her child Ishmael was born after the flesh. Isaac was the child of promise, born to the free woman Sarah. Sarah represents the New Covenant of grace and freedom from the works of the Law, the "Jerusalem that is above" the city of spiritual liberty to which all the children of promise belong.

Hagar the slave was born in the Sinaitic desert, a fitting representative of the spirit of legalism and bondage. Hagar is the covenant of Mount Sinai in Arabia, "which genders to bondage," and "in bondage with her children" (Gal.4:24, 25). Sarah, the freewoman, represents the covenant of grace instituted at Mount Calvary in Jerusalem. Her children are free from the covenant of works. As a result of this new covenant, the old covenant has become obsolete. As the arrival of Isaac - the child of grace and promise, obviated the need for Ishmael, so the arrival of the covenant of grace, sealed with the blood of Christ, obviated the need for the Law. Hence, as Ishmael and his mother must be driven out so too must justification by works must part company. The two cannot live together. As Ishmael mocked Isaac at his weaning, so too the Law and Grace find a great gulf, which no man can cross, fixed between them. They are incompatible. Frederick B. Meyer agrees:

> It is a moral impossibility for the principle of legalism and of faith to co-exist in one heart. Legalism insists on the performance of works - the outward rite of circumcision of the flesh; faith insists on the acceptance of the finished work of Christ - the inward rite of circumcision of the heart. They cannot exist together. Legalism works. Faith rests. Why work towards an objective that is futile when rest in the Savior's work produces the same result. There is no question as to who should go. Ishmael must! The Son abides ever! (*Abraham - Classic Portraits*).

Andrew Jukes concurs:

> If carnal strength succeeds in bearing any fruit, the immediate result is contempt of better things. For the flesh can achieve nothing without being exalted. Sarah, therefore, instead of being "built up," as she had hoped, by Hagar, reaps through her flesh humiliation (*Types of Genesis*).

Symbolically then, this drama teaches us the superiority of faith over works and the supremacy of the covenant of the blood of Christ over that of the Law. We are free from the Law. Therefore let us not be entangled again with the yoke of bondage. For whom the Son has set free is free indeed!

And now, in conclusion, with the message of the allegory still fresh, let us review the practical lessons gleaned from the story of Hagar:

1. We must never attempt to hasten God's promises using our ideas.

Such temptation is greatest when there is delay in fulfillment of a noble promise, for even the wise man acknowledged that "hope deferred makes the heart sick." Instead, let us remember God is not a creature of time, and a thousand years of our time are as but a day with Him. Let us, therefore, be patient and wait on the Lord. He has not forgotten us. The shepherd boy David was anointed king of Israel almost twelve years before all the tribes accepted him as their ruler. And even though he was exiled during most of that period, with a reward out on his head, he patiently waited on God to implement His grand designs. Despite the fate meted out to him, he never ceased to do good for others. Finally, the day came when all of Israel recognized his divine calling and crowned him king.

Abraham, on the other hand, learned that God does not accept substitutes. The son he obtained through the energy of the flesh did not exempt him from waiting for the promise. He still had to wait another fourteen years for the child of promise. And instead of a serene wait, he was forced to endure fourteen years of domestic warfare. A little patience would have spared him from filial disaster and the stain that blotched what may otherwise be described as a stellar life of faith.

2. We must guard against the temptations incident to a new position.

With every new position, and with every blessing comes a responsibility and a caution. God exalts those who are humble but with honor comes along the temptation to pride and haughtiness that in turn leads to arrogance and independence from God. These dangers must be guarded against. We must never cease to depend on God; we must never lean on the arm of flesh; we must never replace prayer with the energy of self; we must never replace the armor of God with carnal weaponry; and we must never believe that we have earned or merited the blessings of God. Any and all such activities are self-defeating. A few words from the battle song, "Stand Up For Jesus" are most appropriate:

Stand up, stand up for Jesus
Stand in His strength alone
The arm of flesh will fail you
Ye dare not trust your own
Put on the gospel armor
And watching unto prayer
Where duty calls or danger
Be never wanting there
- George Webb (1803-1887)

3. When we are tried, as especially so if we were wronged, there is a strong temptation to take matters into our own hands and the almost uncontrollable desire to avenge or vindicate ourselves often blinds us to the truth about our circumstances.

In such moments we resist the impulse to pray, or to wait for divine direction and are driven beyond sense and sensibility, blinded by anger and frustration, and invariably wind up in deeper trouble. But in patience, we must possess our souls. To wiggle in quicksand is to hasten destruction. God knows where we are and will not leave us to die. We are still under construction. God is still at work, molding and fashioning us to be conformed to the image of His Son. And yes, even if we were wronged, He is still able to overrule the evil perpetrated against us for our good and His glory. As Joseph reminded his brothers, "you meant it for evil, but God meant it for good." Surely then, all things will work for good to those who love God and who are called according to His purpose.

4. Sometimes God may require us to return to the point where we turned aside, and it may appear difficult, but He will give us the

grace to do what He asks, and we will receive the blessing if we obey.

The Women's Bible affirms the importance of steadfast obedience to God in times of trials and difficulties:

> Throughout Hagar's life, she experienced estrangement and prejudice as a foreigner, hardship and abuse as a servant, grief and abandonment as an unwed pregnant woman, and hopeless despair on two occasions as she faced imminent death. Yet, despite all these difficulties, Hagar responded to the God who addressed her. She did not get compensation from Sarah and Abraham; her life was never easy, but God did reward her. In the all-seeing God, Hagar found refuge and life" (The Woman's Study Bible, Thomas Nelson).

Despite the emotional roller coaster, we experience in such times, and despite the temptation to take matters into our own hands, we must call on God and wait on Him for direction. He will come to us as He did to Hagar, for He is a God who lives, and sees, and cares.

5. When we feel all alone, friendless, and helpless, we become extremely gullible to the old lie that God has forsaken us because of some sin or transgression on our part.

But remember, even Jesus felt abandoned on the Cross when the Father and His followers were nowhere to be seen. This is a natural human reaction to loneliness. But we must never allow our feelings to dictate a reaction to our circumstances. For the just shall live by faith, and by faith, we must believe our God has His eyes on us, that His angels serve us, and that He will not allow us to be tempted above our ability to bear. Our extremity is His opportunity. He will come just in time to save us, honor His promises, and set us on our feet again.

Even if we are in the transgression, and even if our circumstances were precipitated by our actions, still God is merciful and faithful to forgive us and cleanse us of all unrighteousness. We all make mistakes. We all do and say things that we later regret. But we must be willing to forgive not only ourselves but also our transgressors as well if we expect reciprocal pardon from God.

6. Our lives must be a testimony to grace and faith if we expect to make converts for Christ.

As the redeemed of the Lord we have an obligation to show compassion for others, saving them from fear, and pulling them from the fire before it is too late. How we live is more important than what we say and therefore we must live as true ambassadors of Christ. Men must see the difference in our walk and conversation and be prompted to ask us for the reason for our hope.

7. No matter what happens, or how disappointed we are with those whom we trusted, let us keep our eyes on Jesus and follow Him all the way.

The best of men will let us down. In his dealings with Sarah and Hagar, Abraham displayed nothing to which faith could be properly ascribed. But he must have learned from his mistakes for he later earned the title, "father of faith." We all struggle for perfection, desiring only to serve Christ in good faith. But a heart that is deceitful and desperately wicked governs us. And like the great apostle Paul, we too are deceived and slain by sin and cry out daily for deliverance from this body of death. The path to perfection is lined with stones that cause us to stumble and fall, but always we must rise again, keeping our eyes on Jesus, the Author, and Finisher of our faith. He made it to the end because He maintained focus on the joy that was set before Him and refused to be distracted by the contradiction of sinners. And that is the secret to victory.

Like Hagar, there are millions around the globe who are consciously made to feel inferior by virtue of their color, race, speech, or their cultural heritage and bearing. Some are treated as leprous objects of contempt and scorn because they do not conform to what is deemed acceptable, while others are viewed as objects to be used and abused for the enjoyment and amusement of the privileged. They are underpaid and overworked because those who are supposed to be spiritually enlightened deem them lesser beings. But God knows what you have suffered Hagar, and His eyes are not wide shut but are open to you. Be assured that He is not the One who instructed men to abuse you or to deprive you of common privileges. And neither is He the One who downgraded you according to pigmentation. He cannot be, for you are His child, as special as any other and you need to understand that your life is meant to be meaningful, productive, and abundantly satisfying. John Stott so eloquently reminds us of the Biblical position on human worth and dignity and its importance to the individual:

> Christian teaching on the dignity, nobility, and worth of human beings is of the utmost importance today, partly for the sake of their own self-image and partly for the welfare of society. When human beings are devalued, everything in society goes sour. Women and children are despised; the sick are regarded as a nuisance; and the elderly as a burden; ethnic minorities are discriminated against; capitalism displays its ugliest face; labor is exploited in the mines and factories; criminals are brutalized in prison; opposition opinions are stifled... unbelievers are left to dies in their lostness; there is no freedom, dignity, or carefree joy; human life seems not worth living, because it is scarcely human any longer. But when human beings are valued, because of their intrinsic worth, everything changes: women and children are honored; the sick are cared for and the elderly allowed to live and die with dignity; dissidents are listened to; prisoners are rehabilitated, and minorities protected; workers are given a fair wage, decent working conditions, and a measure of participation in the enterprise; and the gospel is taken to the ends of the earth. Why? Because people matter, because every man, woman, and child has significance as a human person made in the image of God" (*The World's Challenge to the Church, Bibliotheca Sacra, April/June 1988*).

Therefore, abuse and deprecation of any human being is not and cannot be of God, and therefore those who practice it must be of the devil.

So wipe your tears away, Hagar, and remember, though the cards you have been dealt may appear an unfair hand, play them to the best of your ability for the day will come when all inequities will be brought into balance. In the meanwhile, don't let others keep you out of God's program, and do not wait for people to come to an understanding of their errors or to repent of their wrongs and seek your forgiveness. If it takes them fifteen years to realize their errors, are you going to put your life in stasis for all that time? In Hagar's absence from the home, one would think that Sarah had had enough time to contemplate her actions and learn from them so that when Hagar returns things could be different between them. However, it was clear from her subsequent actions that Sarah did not benefit from her time alone.

As I grow older, I realize more and more that this is a cold and unfair world in which we live. Very few people really and truly care about you. This is a reality we must all learn to accept. But equally real is the truth that God cares for each one of us. And on that note, I close with a powerful and relevant passage taken from the writings of J.H Newman:

> God beholds thee, individually, whoever thou art. He "calls thee by name." He knows what is in thee, all thy own peculiar feelings and thoughts, thy disposition and likings, thy strength and thy weakness. He views thee in the day of rejoicing and in the day of sorrow. He sympathizes in thy hopes and in thy temptations. He interests himself in all thy anxieties and remembrances, all the risings and fallings of thy spirit. He has numbered the very hairs of thy head and the cubits of thy stature. He compasses thee around and bears thee in his arms; He takes thee up and sets thee down. He notes thy very countenance, whether smiling or in tears, whether healthful or sickly. He looks tenderly upon thy hands and thy feet; he hears thy voice, the beating of thy heart, and

thy very breathing. Thou art not only his creature; thou art man redeemed and sanctified, His adopted son, favored with a portion of that glory and blessedness which flows from him everlastingly unto the Only Begotten. Thou wast one of those for whom Christ offered up his last prayer and sealed it with his precious blood. What a thought this is, a thought almost too great for our faith!

Cast Thy Burden on the Lord

Thou who art touched with feeling of our woes
Let me on thee my heavy burden cast!
My aching, anguished heart on thee repose,
Leaving with thee this sad mysterious past;
Let me submissively bow and kiss the rod;
Let me "be still, and know that thou art God."

Why should my harassed agitated mind
Go round and round this terrible event?
Striving in vain some brighter side to find,
Some cause why all this anguish has been sent?
Do I indeed that sacred truth believe -
Thou dost not willingly afflict and grieve?

My lovely gourd is withered in an hour!
I droop, I faint beneath the scorching sun;
My Shepherd, lead me to some sheltering bower;
There where Thy little flock "lie down at noon";
Though of my dearest earthly joy bereft
Thou art my portion still; thou, thou, my God, are left.
-Charlotte Elliott

Abigail
Married to a Fool
Story Text: 1 Samuel 25: 18-42

Then Abigail made haste, and took two hundred loaves, and two skins of wine, and five sheep ready dressed, and five measures of parched grain, a hundred clusters of raisins, and two hundred cakes of figs, and laid them on donkeys. And she said to her servants, Go on before me; behold, I come after you. But she told not her husband Nabal. And when Abigail saw David, she hasted, and got off the donkey, and fell before David on her face, and bowed herself to the ground. And fell at his feet, and said, Upon me, my lord, upon me let this iniquity be: and let thy handmaid, I pray thee, speak in thy hearing, and hear the words of thy handmaid. Let not my lord, I pray thee, regard this worthless man, even Nabal: for as his name is, so is he; Nabal is his name, and folly is with him: but I thy handmaid saw not the young men of my lord, whom thou didst send. Now therefore, my lord, as the LORD lives, and as thy soul lives, seeing the LORD hath withheld thee from coming to shed blood, and from avenging thyself with thy own hand, now let thy enemies, and they that seek evil to my lord, be as Nabal.

And now this blessing which thy handmaid hath brought to my lord, let it even be given to the young men that follow my lord. I pray thee, forgive the trespass of thy handmaid: for the LORD will certainly make my lord a sure house; because my lord fights the battles of the LORD, and evil hath not been found in thee all thy days. Yet a man hath risen to pursue thee, and to seek thy soul: but the soul of my lord shall be bound in the bundle of life with the LORD thy God; and the souls of thy enemies, them shall he sling out, as from the middle of a sling. And it shall come to pass, when the LORD shall have done to my lord according to all the good that he hath spoken concerning thee, and shall have appointed thee ruler over Israel; That this shall be no grief to thee, nor offence of heart to my lord, either that thou hast shed blood without cause, or that my lord hath avenged himself: but when the LORD shall have dealt well with my lord, then remember thy handmaid. And David said to Abigail, Blessed be the LORD God of Israel, who sent thee this day to meet me: And blessed be thy advice, and blessed be thou, who hast kept me this day from coming to shed blood, and from avenging myself with my own hand. For in very deed, as the LORD God of Israel lives, who hath kept me back from hurting thee, except thou had hasted and come to meet me, surely there had not been left to Nabal by the morning light any male person. So David received from her hand that which she had brought him, and said to her, Return in peace to thy house; see, I have harkened to thy voice, and have accepted thy person. And Abigail came to Nabal; and, behold, he held a feast in his house, like the feast of a king; and Nabal's heart was merry within him, for he was very drunk: She told him nothing, less or more, until the morning light. But it came to pass in the morning, when the wine had left Nabal, and his wife had told him these things, that his heart died within him, and he became as a stone.

And it came to pass about ten days after, that the LORD smote Nabal, that he died. And when David heard that Nabal was dead, he said, Blessed be the LORD, that hath pleaded the cause of my reproach from the hand of Nabal, and hath kept his servant from evil: for the LORD hath returned the wickedness of Nabal upon his own head. And David sent and talked with Abigail, to take her to himself for a wife. And when the servants of David had come to Abigail to Carmel, they spoke to her, saying, David hath sent us to thee, to take thee to him for a wife. And she arose, and bowed herself on her face to the earth, and said, Behold, let thy handmaid be a servant to wash the feet of the servants of my lord. And Abigail hasted, and arose, and she went after the messengers of David and became his wife.

Abigail, means, "the joy of my father." She was a woman of a good understanding and of a beautiful countenance. She possessed the rare combination of beauty and brains. Unfortunately, her father had given away his "joy" to a livestock farmer named Nabal, a man whose name meant "fool," and who fulfilled the title by living like a fool.

Abigail is first brought into focus as a wife who was sorry for her husband's actions and who wanted to stay judgment against him. Earlier, David's men had approached her husband, asking for some food, citing the fact that they provided protection for his sheepherders and his flocks free of charge. Nabal not only denied their request for help, but he took the liberty of launching a scathing personal attack on David. He falsely accused David of having impure motives for seeking help; that what he really wanted was assistance to lead a revolt against Saul, the king of Israel who sought his life. This accusation aggravated David immensely, and without so much as a second thought, he set out for the home of Nabal to silence the slanderer's tongue. On his way there Abigail, who had subsequently learned of her husband's crass behavior towards David's men and wanted to make amends, intercepted David and apologized for her husband's behavior. As a result of her intercession, David repented of his actions and did not kill her husband.

The lessons learned from Abigail are many and powerful and we will attempt, with the assistance of the Holy Spirit, to glean some comforting truths from this fairy tale drama that will engender faith, hope, and strength in the many women that are bound in indissoluble unions with foolish men.

***

Who is a fool? What constitutes "foolishness?" As finite beings, we possess neither the intellectual capacity nor the spiritual insight to deem anyone foolish, and for these reasons, the Lord issues a severe warning against calling anyone a fool.

But I say to you, that whoever is angry with his brother without a cause shall be in danger of the judgment: and whoever shall say to his brother, Raca, shall be in danger of the council: but whoever shall say, Thou fool, shall be in danger of hell fire (Matthew 5:22).

On the other hand, the omniscient, just, and true Creator does have the wisdom and insight to make such judgments, and we can rest assured that when he calls someone a fool that His judgment is true. The term "fool" as used in Scripture often refers to a lack of wisdom. However, since wisdom has so many different connotations and nuances, there are numerous characteristics of a life of foolishness or folly. In general, a fool is a person who lives his life as if God and the will of God were of no consequence to him. In this regard, God deems foolish the following categories of people:

- ◆ A person who wants nothing to do with God is a fool. The fool says in his heart, "there is no God (Proverbs 14:1). Here is a reference to those who take no account of God and who do not hesitate to show their malice toward "the company of the righteous" (NIV notes Psalm 14). Despite the overwhelming evidence all around, they say, "there is no God." Still there is another interpretation of this verse. You will note the words "*there is*" are italicized, meaning that the translators for grammatical completeness inserted them. If the italicized words "there is" are excluded, the text would read, "The fool says in his heart, no God." That is, such a person believes there is a God, but he wants nothing to do with Him. Either way, a fool is one who denies the existence of God - like the atheist or one who even though he knows of the existence of God, chooses to live independent of Him.
- ◆ A person who is malicious or slanderous is a fool. "He who conceals his hatred has lying lips, and whoever spreads slander is a fool" (Proverbs 10:18). A malicious person plans deceit but disguises it with sweet talk. However, if he succeeds in hiding his feelings, his success is only temporary. The truth will eventually be known, and his own devices will destroy him.

- A person who takes sin lightly is a fool. "Fools mock at making amends for sin" (Proverbs 14:9). To repent is to make amends for sin. A fool makes a mockery of the call to repentance. He finds no reason to repent. He calls good evil and evil good. He walks haughtily before God, unafraid of judgment. He is proud of his perverse way of life and would fight tooth and nail to preserve it.

- A person who despises correction is a fool. "A fool spurns his father's discipline" (Proverbs 15:5). The parameters for fools broaden to include rebellious and disobedient children. They are called foolish because they violate the command of God and in so doing, they rob themselves of its promise - a long and prosperous life. "Children, obey your parents in the Lord, for this is right. Honor your father and mother - which is the first commandment with a promise - that it may go well with you and that you may enjoy long life on the earth" (Ephesians 6: 1-2).

- A person who creates strife and is quick to quarrel is a fool. "It is to a man's honor to avoid strife, but every fool is quick to quarrel" (Proverbs 20:3). An honorable person makes every effort to keep the peace. He sets a guard on his lips and a watch over his mouth. He considers the effects and implications of his words and actions and is careful to ensure that he is not the cause of contention or discord. The fool looks for a fight. He is not happy unless he is quarreling with someone.

- A person who trusts in himself is a fool. "He who trusts in himself is a fool" (Proverbs 28:26). The Scripture teaches that the unregenerate heart is "deceitful and desperately wicked." That is, until the application of divine grace, the heart of man is gravely ill and incurable. It is great folly then to trust in the human heart for wisdom and guidance. The wise man does not lean on his own understanding but looks to the Lord for guidance.

- A person who is dishonest and unjust is a fool. "Like a partridge that hatches eggs it did not lay is the man who gains riches by unjust means. When his life is half gone, they will desert him, and in the end, he will prove to be a fool"

(Jeremiah 17:11). Those who amass riches by using unjust means are likened to a partridge. This bird would hatch the eggs of another bird and fool itself into believing that the chicks are hers. She is soon disappointed when she finds the offspring going off with their real mother. Even so, wealth unjustly acquired is taken away and its hoarder becomes the fool.

♦ A hypocrite is a fool. Then the Lord said to him (the Pharisee), "Now then, you Pharisees clean the outside of the cup and dish, but inside you are full of greed and wickedness. You foolish people!" (Luke 11:39-40). This definition of fools encapsulates those who depend on outward "works of righteousness which they have done" to give them a ticket to eternal life. When they give, they seek the acknowledgment of others; when they pray and fast, they must be seen and heard by men; they have a form of godliness but deny the power thereof; they beckon men to enter the kingdom of God but they themselves would not enter in; they pay tithes but overlook the weightier matters of judgment like the showing of mercy. And because many are deceived by their hypocrisy, they believe that God is also fooled.

♦ A person who is indifferent to God's word is a fool. "But everyone who hears these words of mine and does not put them into practice is like a foolish man who built his house upon the sand" (Matthew 7:24-27). The man who hears the Word of God and does not put it into practice is like the man who knows there is a God but wants nothing to do with Him. He too is a fool.

♦ A person who does not prepare for eternity is a fool. "But God said to him (the rich farmer), you fool! This very night your life will be demanded from you. Then who will get what you have prepared for yourself?" (Luke 12:20). The story is told of a king who, on his deathbed, summoned the court jester to his bedside to honor him for years of faithful service. On his arrival the king presented to him a golden wand, honoring him as the greatest fool ever for he had never failed to cheer up the king in times of sadness. The king then asked the jester to make a tour of the country to see if he can find a fool greater than himself and charged him that if he does, then he must turn the wand over to that person. The king then bade him a tearful farewell saying that he should not expect to find him upon his return, for he was taking a far journey from which there is no return. The fool then asked the king if he was prepared for his journey seeing it was a one-way trip to a faraway place. The king sadly shook his head saying he was not prepared for this journey. Shocked, the fool turned to the king and said, "O King, you are taking a far journey from which there is no return and yet you have not prepared for that journey? Here, you take this wand from me, for I have found a fool greater than myself."

Alas, how many like the king will scream in Hell for all eternity, "I knew all too well that one day I must take a far journey from which there is no return, but I never took time to prepare my soul for the journey beyond the river of Death. What a fool I have been!"

All men without the knowledge of God are fools. "At one time we too were foolish, disobedient, deceived, and enslaved by all kinds of passions and pleasures. We lived in malice and envy, being hated, and hating one another" (Titus 3:3). This "knowledge of God" refers to more than a mere head knowledge of God. It refers to a heart experience of God. Without that heart knowledge of God, it matters not how wise in the world men might be, as far as God is concerned, their knowledge is foolishness. In the words of Johann Georg von Zimmermann, "they are children with edged weapons, they hurt themselves, and put others in pain. The half-learned is more dangerous than the simpleton." Indeed, if one were to obtain the world of knowledge without the knowledge of God, he would still be less than half-learned. God is Creator, Owner, Giver, and Sustainer of all things. In Him, we live, and move, and have our being. Without Him, we can do nothing. How then can a life that is lived apart from Him be deemed anything other than foolish? Concerning all fools, the Bible tells us that God has no pleasure in them (Ecclesiastes 5:4); that they shall not stand in His presence (Psalms 5:5); and that they shall finally come to shame and ruin (Proverbs 3:35).

We see then that the term "fool" is broadened to include many, including the worldly-wise that live apart from God. It is in light of this expanded definition of a fool that we will consider the subject, "Married to a Fool." Abigail was married to one type of fool you might be bound to another. Having then defined the term "fool" as God used it, we will now proceed to the lessons we can learn from the beautiful Abigail.

***

1. Everyone can make a difference.

David was a man of much self-restraint. He waited patiently on the Lord to establish him on the throne of Israel. He endured death threats and persecutions and could on several occasions have legitimately killed Saul in self-defense and hastened his ascent to the throne but chose not to "touch the Lord's anointed." When he returned to Ziklag and saw it burnt to the ground and the women and children were taken captive by the enemy, his immediate reaction was to summon the "ephod," that part of the High Priest's garment containing a stone and which was used to enquire of the Lord the course of action to be taken in a particular situation, to be brought to him. Most warriors would pursue the enemy without a meeting with their war council, but David sought divine direction. He was indeed a "man after God's heart." But now Nabal had stretched his patience to the limit with insulting words and David could no longer hold his peace. He was going to avenge himself. And had it not been for the timely interruption for Abigail, he would have executed Nabal and cast a dark shadow on his illustrious career.

Abigail hastened to meet him and apologize for her husband's crude behavior. Remarkably so, she thanked him for not killing her husband. She reminded David that he was a soldier of the Lord and that the Lord will fight his battles for him. She reminded him of the future when he would be king. Would he want to tarnish his reputation over a simple misfit like Nabal? Her reasoning brought David back to himself. He said to her, "Blessed be the Lord, the God of Israel, which hath sent thee this day to meet me: And blessed be thy wisdom, and blessed be thou, which hast kept me this day from blood-guiltiness, and from avenging myself with my own hand."

Whether they be small and in captivity, like Naaman's maid, or subtle and gentle, like Abigail, every person can make a lasting difference in the lives of others and impact history in a way unimaginable. Because of the intercession of a little captive maid, Naaman was saved, and a heathen nation was given a powerful gospel witness. And because of the intercession of Abigail, the man who was to be king was saved from shedding more blood and from jeopardizing the throne of Israel. At the time it may not have seemed to Abigail that what she did was of any significance other than saving her husband, but as the years went by, and as Israel flourished under its greatest king, she knew for sure that the smallest act of grace and kindness has its rewards. She was "faithful in a few things" and now, sitting in the palace beside the king, she had become a "ruler of many cities." Abigail reminds us to be faithful in the little things God asks of us, remembering that in those little things we can make a world of a difference to men and nations.

2. We must be sensitive to the workings of Providence.

As we journey through the history of the Bible, we see God working effectively with every kind of instrument available to Him at the time of need. He worked with the rod of Moses to bring deliverance to the Hebrews. He worked with the aid of a donkey to speak sense to a materialistic prophet. He worked with a shepherd's sling to kill a giant enemy and restore the integrity of a nation. He worked with the "jawbone of an ass" to route the Philistines. He worked with a pot of oil to pay off the debts of a widowed woman. He worked with five loaves and two fishes to satiate the hunger of a multitude. And He worked with handkerchiefs to transmit healing to the sick.

We also see Him working with little people, captive people, ignorant people, ostracized people, hated people, scorned people, and condemned people. We must understand that all things were made by God and for God and therefore He has the right to use anything and anyone for His pleasure and purpose. That is the Creator's right. Subconsciously we do not believe that it is possible for us to be blessed by sinners or be ministered to by others we deem to be unqualified. As such we lose out on God.

The apostle Paul, a man who before his conversion "wreaked havoc" on the church, and who referred to himself as the "chief of sinners," made note of the type of instruments found in God's toolbox.

> But God hath chosen the foolish things of the world to confound the wise, and God hath chosen the weak things of the world to confound the things which are mighty; and base things of the world, and things which are despised, hath God chosen, yea, and things which are not, to bring to nothing things that are (1 Corinthians 1:27-28).

Look at these instruments in the divine toolbox - Foolish things! Weak things! Base things! Despised things! Non-existent things! And why does God use such instruments? The answer is found in the following verse: So "that no flesh should glory in His presence" (v.29).

We are often robbed of many blessings, either because we fail to understand the way in which God works or we do not recognize the instruments He uses in the furtherance of His purposes. Had David looked at the person of Abigail, her station in life, her religious experience, and her qualifications, he would have dismissed her without a word. But he stopped and listened to Abigail. He knew God once used him when he was an innocent skinny shepherd boy to overcome an ominous giant who drove fear into the hearts of an army of mighty soldiers. If Saul had looked upon his stature and qualifications and prevented him from dueling with Goliath, the history of the nation of Israel would have taken a different course. Yet, despite the fact he was not a soldier, Saul, recognizing he was there at that moment by divine design, sent him to do battle with Goliath, saying, "Go, and the Lord be with thee."

David was prevented from making a terrible mistake and only so because he recognized that "the Lord God hath sent thee to meet me this day" and "keep me from blood guiltiness." Let us also ask God to send men and women to keep us from making terrible mistakes; and that when He does, to help us to recognize that it is the "God of Israel which hath sent thee" to meet us and keep us from error.

3. Abigail reminds us that vengeance belongs to God.

We are often tempted to avenge ourselves, especially when our ego is hurt. David was very conscious of the fact that he was already anointed king of Israel and, gathering from the semi-prophetic words of Abigail in verses 28-30, it was obvious that the whole nation of Israel knew he was the king in waiting. So, as far as David was concerned, he deserved respect.

But along comes Nabal and he answers David's reasonable request for assistance with contempt and derision. Already a fugitive from the madman Saul, facing death each day, it did not take much to push him over the edge. And Nabal did just that. David knew that because Saul had declared war on him everyone felt free to stomp on him. He knew that if Saul had been at peace with him, Nabal would never have treated him the way he did. Instead, he would have done exactly as his wife later did - bring him gifts and well wishes and treat him as a king. But the pompous Nabal made matters worse when he openly belittled David in the presence of his men. And David could not allow that to happen. If Nabal did not wish to offer help, the least he could have done was to say No and leave it at that. But he was a self-appointed judge, jury, and executioner on David's case. And David was determined to teach him a lesson. Driven by vengeance, he rushed to the house of Nabal with a plan to avenge himself. Not only was he going to silence Nabal's tongue forever, but he was also going to kill all his men. How vengeance blinds even the noblest of us!

As David hastened on his vengeance mission to Nabal's home, Abigail intercepted him and reminded him of whom he is. She reminded him that he was a man who always trusted the Lord to fight his battles for him, and how God had never failed him, and she explained why he must not allow a foolish man to aggravate him into doing something he will regret for the rest of his life. She reminded him that forgiveness is better than revenge. She reminded him that if he expects to obtain mercy from God, he must learn to show mercy to man; and that if he will not forgive men their trespasses will God forgive him his trespasses. She reminded him that revenge never satisfies; that it never atones; that it never appeases the conscience; that its sweetness is afterward turned into bitterness; and that it will trail him like a wild beast all the days of his life. She reminded him that forgiveness is divine, and it is the glory of great men to pass by offenses done to them, and in the end, those who forgive will be spared from a heart of reproach and a lifetime of regret.

Abigail was practical in her reasoning, prophetic in her presentation, philosophical in her argument, and poignant in her poise, as she withstood David. Continuing boldly, she pointed out to him that to kill Nabal is to "shed blood without cause." In effect, she said to David that if he were to kill her husband based on what had transpired, he would not be better than her husband, but like him, just another fool. Had she attempted that kind of argument with her husband he would have leveled her with a blow. But David was not like her husband. In the presence of all his warriors, he humbled himself, and acknowledged his error and foolishness, repeating almost "verbatim" the words of Abigail. He said to Abigail, "I am well pleased with thee and what thou hast said." He forgave Nabal and as if to confirm that his actions were pleasing to God, ten days later, the Lord himself "smote Nabal that he died."

Whenever we are tempted to seek vengeance or to justify retaliation, let us remember the story of David and Abigail and stay our anger. Even if we do return vengeance on the heads of those who wrong us, we will afterward be faced with an accusing conscience and a condemning heart. Suddenly it will occur to us that we are no different from our accusers. Remember, vengeance is the Lord's, therefore let us leave our accusers to Him. When he takes care of them our hands will be free of blood, our hearts will remain undefiled, our character unblemished, and like David, "the Lord will certainly make us a sure house...for evil will not be found in us in all our days." Let us learn to forgive others for their trespasses even as we expect God to forgive us for our trespasses against Him. Abigail taught that we should not avenge ourselves (v.26, 31), David agreed (v.33), and the Lord confirmed the word (v.39).

4. We must make haste when God calls.

On hearing of Nabal's arrogant behavior towards David's men and the impending consequences of that attitude, Abigail could have waited for David to come to her house and then hope to appease his wrath. But she did not take that chance. Instead, she hastened to meet him (v. 18) with her gifts of repentance. She brought to him all that he had initially asked for and she sought his forgiveness. A few days later, after her husband died and David proposed marriage, she accepted and "hasted...and became his wife" (v.42).

In this regard, we learn from Abigail the importance of hastening to the Lord to avert judgment for our wrongdoing against Him, and to hasten to take up His offer to become a part of His bride. Abigail did not procrastinate in either of these matters. She hastened to repentance as a sinner, and she hastened to marriage as a redeemed saint. What a message this is to saints and sinners alike. The sinner must know he cannot afford to delay salvation. Delay is dangerous. Many with noble intentions populate the screaming halls of hell. They knew they needed protection from the "Avenger of Blood," but waited and waited until it was too late. If you are not saved, don't delay. Hasten to Christ, the Son of David, and seek His forgiveness for your sins. He will "receive your hand," and say to you, "I have hearkened to thy voice, and have accepted thy person" (v.35).

Christ calls the redeemed to his side into a union and bond as strong as marriage. He wants you to be His bride for all eternity. But you must be without spot and blemish, pure in heart and desire, and you must hasten to His side and remain at His side always. What a glorious privilege indeed it is to be saved! Still, what inexplicable love to be called to be the bride of the King of Kings and Lord of Lord for all the ages to come! Yet, that is the privilege of all.

5. We must focus on the big picture – the future.

Abigail pointed David to the future when he would be king. Would he want this ugly episode to trial him like a wild beast all the days of his life? Would he want those ugly memories to be interjected into every conversation? Would he want his children to hear this episode of his life as a bedtime story? In effect, she regulated his present actions by redirecting his vision to the future.

Likewise, Jesus, our heavenly David, endured the present shame of the cross and the contradiction of sinners because He looked forward to the "joy that was set before Him," when He will be "seated at the right hand of God, making intercession for us," and "bringing many sons unto glory." Similarly, the apostle Paul was able to endure suffering, trials, cruel mocking, nakedness, perils, and dangers, because he looked ahead to the "crown of righteousness" that awaited him. And the men and women of faith listed in Hebrews, chapter 11, endured to death because they looked for an eternal city whose maker and builder is God. They possessed telescopic vision, seeing beyond the visible, temporal and tangible, to the invisible, eternal, and truly satisfying.

If we do the same, if we think about the repercussions of our actions as they unravel into the future, much of what we do and say will be audited before release. And we will be spared the consequence in later years when those seeds would have germinated and matured. Oh yes! The principle of sowing and reaping is inflexible. Much of what we reap presently are the fruits of what was previously sowed, and over that, we have little control. The law must be executed. The swung pendulum must return. However, through this same inflexible law, we do have some advantage, some measure of control over our future. We dictate our future by what seeds we are prepared to sow now. If we sow well, we will come to the end of our days with happy rewards. If we sow evil, we will come to the end of our lives miserable, empty, and bitter. We can determine that end! We are children of eternity, so let us live with long-term goals in mind. If you must endure trials and hardship, then remember that this "present light affliction" cannot be compared to the glory that shall be revealed in you in your future state. If you must suffer for the cause of the Lord Jesus Christ and His kingdom, then you must remember that those who "suffer with Him shall reign with Him."

And if it appears that all your labors for Him go unnoticed, unappreciated, and without reward, do not despair, for God is not unrighteous to forget your work and labor of love which you have shown towards His name. Keep focused on the never-ending joy that awaits you in the land where there is no heartache, no pain, no sadness, no sorrow, and no death. And when you are so focused you too will be able to endure your cross and patiently run the race that is set before you. The songwriter says it well:

Turn your eyes upon Jesus,
Look full in His wonderful face
And the things of earth will grow strangely dim,
In the light of His glory and grace.

6. Intercessory prayer works.

Because of Abigail's intercession, her family as well as those in her employment was saved. Likewise, when Abraham prayed, Lot was delivered; when David killed Goliath, he saved the nation of Israel; when Rahab aided the spies, she and her household were saved from the destruction that visited Jericho; when Cornelius believed the gospel, his entire household was saved. Intercession saves more than the intercessor. It saves those in its ambiance as well.

Abigail's intercession went beyond words. She offered herself as the scapegoat for her husband's iniquity (v. 24), even though he was, in her own words, "a worthless man." What a powerful symbolism of the Lord Jesus Christ who offered Himself for the sins of the world of "worthless" people in whom there is only folly. He became a substitute for our sins, taking the punishment for it as though it was His own. The prophet Isaiah said, "He was wounded for our transgressions, He was bruised for our iniquities, the chastisement of our peace was upon Him, and by His stripes, we are healed."

Let us intercede for the lost and the tempted and let us be willing to substitute ourselves if needs be as a scapegoat for their iniquity. In the end, it will be worth it all.

7. The just must live by faith.

Abigail lived by faith. She was fully aware that "faith without works is dead," so she put foot to her faith and went with gifts of repentance to meet the advancing David. She believed that her gifts of repentance would be accepted and that her intercession would prevail. While entreating the mercy of David she implied that what she asked of him was already done. She turned to David, an angry man with a drawn sword ready to decapitate the heads of her household, and said to him, "The Lord hath withholden thee." How could David have pursued this mad course after such a constraining and prophetic statement of faith? Abigail's faith obtained amnesty for her household and stayed the hand of judgment.

Another aspect of her faith that is worthy of note is her acceptance of David's marriage proposal after the death of her husband. Her marriage to him was an act of faith. Remember, at the time David asked her to marry him he was a renegade and fugitive, without a home and with no certainty about his future. And considering the fact she was just released from a lifelong union with a foolish man, she really needed faith to enter another with a man who only a little earlier was about to have her decapitated. But her faith was in the promises of God that were made to this man and his seed. Likewise, those who accept Christ, the "Root out of dry ground" from whom we hid our faces, must be willing to suffer with Him, by faith believing that hereafter they shall reign with Him.

8. We have an obligation to uphold our marriage vows even if married to a fool.

Like Abigail, many precious women are married to fools like Nabal. The great English preacher, Frederick Meyer, observed: "It is remarkable how many Abigails get married to Nabals. God-fearing women, tender and gentle in their sensibilities, high-minded and noble in their ideals, become tied in an indissoluble union with men for whom they can have no true affinity, even if they have not an unconquerable repugnance."

For some, custom, culture, and tradition have forced men like Nabal on them, while deceit, flattery, promises, or mitigating circumstances were the matchmakers for others. Yet, despite the origin of the union, the result is the same - daily abuse, crushed hopes, ruined dreams, and unfulfilled ambitions. The will is trampled, individuality is lost, self-esteem plunges to depths unreachable, and life morphs into mere existence, not much different from that of the baser forms of life. The will to live is jeopardized. Suicide becomes a friendly possibility. Life dangles precariously on strands of innate support that say we are life-affirming, and we must not quit our station in life, and that as long as there is life, there is hope.

Abigail wound up with the misfortune of being tied in an indissoluble union with a husband with whom she had no affinity whatsoever and who possessed an unconquerable repugnance. This man did not deserve her, but as custom would have it, she had no choice in the matter and was forced to play the hand she had been dealt. Like many wives today, she was just an asset, a glorified slave, a receptacle for her husband's lusts, a punching bag for him to vent his anger and frustration. She lived in fear from morning to night and endured daily embarrassments, just hoping, always hoping that someday her husband would change. I imagined she made his favorite meals, kept her home well, and did everything right just so that he would be pleased. But he was never pleased, never appreciative, never encouraging, never satisfied. What was she to do? What options are open to women who find themselves in her plight? Abigail endured. She did not quit her station in life. She continued to give her best, refusing to let her character be blemished by an idiot, yet hoping that by her life and goodness she may turn his heart of stone into a heart of flesh and blood.

Her plight is a dire warning to young women who will soon come to the threshold of marriage. You may not be forced into a union by custom or culture, but you can be seduced into a lifelong affair with terror and abuse if you are not careful and prayerful. Many men are masters in the art of flattery, and some are master illusionists, showing you what does not exist. Beware of them if you seek to avoid a lifetime of pain. Don't allow the wealth and worldly goods of the Nabals to blind your sense of reason and good judgment. Alexander Pope once said, "Fools rush in where angels fear to tread." Don't be a fool. Indeed, many Abigails knew they were rushing into a potentially dangerous affair but proceeded nevertheless, hoping somehow to influence changes in their Nabals.

Alas, they rushed in easily but found change difficult and escape virtually impossible.

Let us remember that prevention is still better than cure and that prevention is facilitated through fervent prayer, patient waiting, and heavenly wisdom. As fate would have it, Nabal died shortly after, leaving Abigail free to remarry. You may not be that lucky!

9. There is a time to break the rules.

According to the divine arrangement, the husband is the head of the home. That means he is entrusted with the spiritual destiny of his home (Joshua. 24:15). But if he fails to assume and carry out that responsibility, his spiritual authority is set aside, and it is time for his wife to take charge.

David's men had come to Nabal with a reasonable request. They asked for food in return for providing valuable protection services for his men and sheep. But Nabal flatly refused them any food. On hearing of the matter, Abigail immediately acted to remedy the situation, fully aware of the risk of having her husband find out. She knew the right thing and did it courageously. Afterward, she told Nabal what she had done, and he became so angry, that his blood pressure rose, he got a stroke and died. Was she wrong to act without her husband's consent? Should she have told him she was going to help David, knowing fully well he would prevent her from doing so? Or should she have gone along with Nabal's refusal to help and just blame the whole situation on him? The results proved she made the right decision. God vindicated her actions. David repented and the Lord smote her husband.

10. Only our heavenly David can truly set us free.

The drama that unfolded between David, Nabal, and Abigail, has a deeper significance. It previsions the drama that unfolded between the Law, those held in bondage to the Law, and to salvation by Grace, as offered through Jesus Christ, the Son of David. In this regard, we note the following similarities:

I: The demands of the law could not be satisfied.

Consider Abigail's nightmarish bondage. Her husband was churlish in character and childish in concepts. His days began with a hangover and ended in wine and merriment. He lived to himself and for himself. Jesus must have had him in mind when he spoke the parable of the rich fool who thought it was well with his soul simply because his barns were filled with grain. It mattered not how hard Abigail tried, she simply could not please this man. He was exacting, cruelly demanding, a relentless taskmaster, never commending the good that she did but always first to criticize her for omissions and shortcomings. His demands were insatiable.

The Law too was harsh, but its harshness was well-intentioned. It was our schoolmaster to bring us to Christ. Its method was to reveal our sinfulness and our inability to meet the standard of holiness required by God, thereby creating in us a yearning for a Savior. Thus, because the Law condemned us as sinners it was for an eternally good cause. It brought us to our heavenly David who gave us peace and salvation. Similarly, had it not been for Nabal's abusive behavior, Abigail would never have come to know the happiness and fulfillment her David would bring. This of course does not excuse Nabal's behavior, but it does teach us that the All-powerful, Almighty, and omniscient God is able to work all our negative experiences for our ultimate good and gain. Remember what Joseph said to his brothers who had sold him into slavery? He said to them, "You meant it for evil, but God meant it for good, for He hath sent me before you to preserve life." His brothers were not excused for their actions, but God was able to overturn the evil they intended for the salvation of nations, including the evildoers themselves. So too, God was able to turn Nabal's abuse of his wife for her ultimate good. Before leaving this point, it is necessary to highlight the efficacy of the salvation offered by the Lord Jesus Christ. As our heavenly David is greater than the earthly David, so is His salvation. David saved the life of Abigail, but our David saved our souls. David saved Abigail from temporal distress, but we are saved from the eternal distress of spiritual death.

II: The only way out of legalism is death to self.

So long as Nabal was alive, Abigail suffered under his exacting demands. Divorce was not an option. She endured life daily, hoping for a change. But there was none. Nabal was the same, day after day. No amount of counseling sessions and seminars helped. He was adamant, unyielding, unchanging, static, legalistic, not even accepting the fact that he needed help. To him everyone else was wrong. They needed an attitude adjustment, not him. As fate would have it, Nabal died shortly after, and his death opened the way for Abigail to marry David. Likewise, despite the harshness of the Law, there is no way out of it other than death. For he that is dead is released from the Law. At Calvary, Jesus met the demands of the Law through His death and thereby released us from its oppression. Now we are free to be "married to another, even to Him who is raised from the dead" (Romans 7:4).

III: There is life and liberty in the "Son of David."

The story ended like a fairy tale. The unrepentant idiot Nabal died. The heroic future king married the free Abigail. Virtue triumphs over evil once again. And they lived happily after. So too ends all of God's doings. There is no unhappy ending for those who have found their "Son of David," Jesus Christ as their Savior, Lord, and eventual Bridegroom. They too will live forever in the Paradise of God.

Conclusion

Many Abigails - beautiful, fair, kind, and gentlewomen - find themselves bound up in unions with Nabals - foolish spouses. Some have had Nabals forced upon them while others have been deceived, temporarily blinded by love and the promise of a happy life. And these unions may have become indissoluble for various reasons – broken marriage vows, childless partnerships, and cultural and religious commitments are a few. Yet, it matters not so much how the union came to being or why it is being held together; the fact is that God recognizes the marriage and "what God hath joined together let not man put asunder." So what are the Abigails to do?

You are to remember that even in your "captivity," you can still be of service to God and His kingdom; and that your abiding faithfulness will result in the salvation of many others. It would help if you remained faithful to your spouse. You must recognize that God is faithful, and He will not suffer you to be tempted above your ability to endure and that He can make a way when there seems to be no way out. You must maintain an abiding faith in the goodness and power of Almighty God to change your situation for the better, and remember that "all things (good and bad) work together for good to them that love the Lord..." You must continue to pray for your spouse. Intercede fervently for their salvation and believe that God can save your spouse. For there is none so far fallen that God cannot reach them. The Bible says, "His hands are not shortened that He cannot save." The grace of God knows no limits. He can save to the "uttermost them that come to...Him." Indeed, He saved the deceiver Jacob and made him a prince with God. He saved Saul, the destroyer of the Church, and made him the greatest builder of the Church. From the "chief of sinners," he was made the "chief of apostles." He saved ignorant and unlearned fishers and made them men of power who summoned the world's attention. He saved adulterous women and made them monuments of grace. Abigail also reminds us never to seek revenge, for "vengeance is the Lord's."

Finally, you must remember that you are espoused to your heavenly David, who will one day return to take you to be with Him forevermore to His home where there will be no more abuse but where you will be loved and cherished and made to share in an ongoing love affair with the Son of God who loved you and gave Himself for you. As you focus on the day when your heavenly Bridegroom shall appear and take you into an eternal union of unending bliss, you will be able to endure your temporal discomfort, for this "light affliction" cannot be compared with the glory that shall be revealed in you.

For those who do not know Christ, your plight is worse. For only the heavenly David can set you free. But you must hasten to Him with your gifts of repentance. Do not delay for one moment, for each passing second brings the Avenger of blood closer to you. Go out yourself to meet Him and "kiss the Son lest He be angry." Ask His forgiveness, and you will find, no matter how grave your trespass might be, He will abundantly pardon you. You will discover that repentance opens the door to a new start with God and that it avails you the strength and faith necessary to deal with your problems. You will soon learn that fairy tales are not wishful fantasies but that they can come through and that when Christ comes into your life, "old things are passed away and behold, all things become new." You will experience true love and inherit the sure hope of being carried away to your mansion in the sky where, with your heavenly David, you will live forevermore, happily ever after!

Hannah
Weep No More
Story Text: 1 Samuel 1:1-28

Now there was a certain man of Ramathaim Zophim, of the mountains of Ephraim, and his name was Elkanah the son of Jeroham, the son of Elihu, the son of Tohu, the son of Zuph, an Ephraimite. And he had two wives: the name of one was Hannah and the name of the other Peninnah. Peninnah had children, but Hannah had no children. This man went up from his city yearly to worship and sacrifice to the Lord of hosts in Shiloh. Also, the two sons of Eli, Hophni, and Phinehas, the priests of the Lord, were there. And whenever the time came for Elkanah to make an offering, he would give portions to Peninnah his wife, and to all her sons and daughters. But to Hannah, he would give a double portion, for he loved Hannah, although the Lord had closed her womb. And her rival also provoked her severely, to make her miserable, because the Lord had closed her womb. So it was, year by year, when she went up to the house of the Lord, that she provoked her; therefore she wept and did not eat.

Then Elkanah her husband said to her, "Hannah, why do you weep? Why do you not eat? And why is your heart grieved? Am I not better to you than ten sons?"

So Hannah arose after they had finished eating and drinking in Shiloh. Now Eli the priest was sitting on the seat by the doorpost of the tabernacle of the Lord. And she was in bitterness of soul and prayed to the Lord and wept in anguish. Then she made a vow and said, "O Lord of hosts, if You will indeed look on the affliction of Your maidservant and remember me, and not forget Your maidservant, but will give Your maidservant a male child, then I will give him to the Lord all the days of his life, and no razor shall come upon his head."

And it happened, as she continued praying before the Lord, that Eli watched her mouth. Now Hannah spoke in her heart; only her lips moved, but her voice was not heard. Therefore Eli thought she was drunk. So Eli said to her, "How long will you be drunk? Put your wine away from you!"

But Hannah answered and said, "No, my lord, I am a woman of sorrowful spirit. I have drunk neither wine nor intoxicating drink but

have poured out my soul before the Lord. Do not consider your maidservant a wicked woman, for out of the abundance of my complaint and grief I have spoken until now."
Then Eli answered and said, "Go in peace, and the God of Israel grant your petition which you have asked of Him."
And she said, "Let your maidservant find favor in your sight." So the woman went her way and ate, and her face was no longer sad.
Then they rose early in the morning and worshiped before the Lord and returned and came to their house at Ramah. And Elkanah knew Hannah his wife, and the Lord remembered her. So it came to pass in the process of time that Hannah conceived and bore a son, and called his name Samuel, saying, "Because I have asked for him from the Lord."
Now the man Elkanah and all his house went up to offer to the Lord the yearly sacrifice and his vow. But Hannah did not go up, for she said to her husband, "Not until the child is weaned; then I will take him, that he may appear before the Lord and remain there forever."
So Elkanah her husband said to her, "Do what seems best to you; wait until you have weaned him. Only let the Lord establish His word." Then the woman stayed and nursed her son until she had weaned him.
Now when she had weaned him, she took him up with her, with three bulls, one ephah of flour, and a skin of wine, and brought him to the house of the Lord in Shiloh. And the child was young. Then they slaughtered a bull and brought the child to Eli. And she said, "O my lord! As your soul lives, my lord, I am the woman who stood by you here, praying to the Lord. For this child, I prayed, and the Lord has granted me my petition which I asked of Him. Therefore I also have lent him to the Lord; as long as he lives, he shall be lent to the Lord." So they worshiped the Lord there.

Our story occurs approximately 1,000 years before the birth of Christ. It took place during the autumn festival that the Hebrews celebrated annually and was generally a family affair. Many will make the journey to Shiloh to celebrate and recommit themselves to the Lord of the harvest. It is in this spirit that Elkanah and his family understood the yearly pilgrimage (*Hayes, 1 & 2 Samuel, p. 16*). Against the backdrop of celebration, the sadness of Hannah is made even worse by the needling of a haughty Peninah, the other wife of Elkanah.

Polygamy was not uncommon in Old Testament times. This is not to say it was divinely sanctioned. But for the Hebrews, it served several purposes. Since life beyond the grave was vague, children were the means of perpetuating the family name and vicariously, one's own personality (*Hayes, p.16*). Also, in Biblical times one's children were often the only form of social security available for old age. Polygamy also ensured protection for women members of the community. Daughters were best protected in marriage (*Akroyd, p. 19*).

It is likely that Elkanah married Hannah first, but since he could not obtain children from her, he married Peninnah (a woman with rich hair) to remove reproach from his family. Apparently, a bitter rivalry ensued between the two wives about their ability to bear children and Peninnah used her advantage to taunt Hannah about her barrenness. Yet, despite Hannah's condition, it was evident that Elkanah loved her more than he did Peninnah. Arguably it was his special affection for Hannah that may have fueled the daily tensions between the two women. As Walter Brueggemann observed, "Hannah's barrenness overrides the power of Elkanah's love. The outcome is a provoked woman, abused by her rival, Peninah, more vexed by Yahweh's foreclosure of her future. Hannah's response to her trouble is depression, grief, and loss of appetite" (*W. Brueggemann, p.13*)

In her distress, Hannah prayed to the Lord for a son and promised to dedicate him to Yahweh. Eli, the priest, who at first mistook her praying as drunken behavior, gave her request his blessing. Hannah's mood changed noticeably after this (*WBC, p.4*). She became pregnant and gave birth to Samuel. After she had weaned the child, she brought him up to Shiloh with the appropriate offerings. And because it was Yahweh who had granted her request, she dedicated her son to Him and left him in Shiloh.

As Ralph Klein observed, the motif of a barren wife who is given a child by Yahweh and whose child plays an important role occurs frequently in the Old Testament. The barrenness of Sarah until the birth of Isaac, of Rachel until the birth of Joseph and Benjamin, of the wife of Manoah until the birth of Samson, are a few that come to mind (*WBC, p.4*). In the New Testament, the motif is extended with Elizabeth giving birth to John the Baptist. Klein noted that the frequent presence of a rival who bears children and uses her fertility to irritate the barren woman lends poignancy to these stories (*p.4*). Again, Hagar and Sarah, Leah, and Rachel come to mind. Now it was Peninah and Hannah's turn. In all this, we must not underestimate the value of an Israelite woman having a child. John Hayes rightly suggests that because of the medical techniques available today to deal with infertility, modern readers are not always caught up in the same tension of this drama as earlier generations might have been. In addition, children, though loved and cherished, are no longer considered a means of a family's economic survival, and often the temptation is to read the plight of Hannah with benign indulgence (*Hayes, p.16*).

Beyond her infertility, Hannah was a typical representative of oppressed women of all times (*Robinson, p.13*). She was discriminated against by a male chauvinistic Israelite society, treated as part of a man's possessions, and not his equal. Polygamy was a consequence of this discrimination. The fact that she was barren only added social stigma to her cache of problems. Thus, it is understandable why the birth of a child would initiate such an unmitigated celebration. The deepest yearning of a woman had been fulfilled by a miracle. The woman's worth, dignity, and rightful place with her husband are restored. Hannah must sing!

The story commences on a sad note. We see Hannah on the stair of the temple, crying bitterly. It was tough already on an Israelite woman not to be able to bear children. To be taunted by other women only aggravated the pain. So intense was her agony of soul that she could not express her pain in legible sentences. The only language she knew was that of tears. She groaned and cried, day and night, week after week, to the point where she appeared as an inebriated woman speaking gibberish. The reaction of the priest implied that she might have been an embarrassment to the religious establishment. Fortunately, Hannah stood her ground and prevailed with God. As Hayes noted, the electricity in this story is generated by that paradox between the barrenness of the womb and the fertility of her spirit (*Hayes, p.16*). She obtained the desire of her heart, a son she named Samuel. He would grow up to be one of the most distinguished and revered prophets of Israel.

As we study this brief but poignant story, we would be amiss if we are unable to glean the principles that moved Hannah from desperate barrenness to joyful exuberance. She was barren at the beginning but fruitful in the end. How did she move from blight to blessing? How was she able to turn the bad hand dealt her into a winning deck? If we zero in on the principles that moved her from one end of the spectrum to the other, we will arm ourselves with the keys that will equip us to do likewise. There are eight keys on the bunch that must be used to open the door of blessing.

1: Understand that fatalism is not biblical.

Some people resign their lives to fate, believing it was their destiny to suffer. The term "born loser" quickly comes to mind. For example, the Hindu philosophy of reincarnation and associated doctrine of karma would have condemned Hannah to a life of barrenness. They would argue it is her karma to remain childless. And then theories on causality would have abounded. Maybe she killed a child in her previous existence. Maybe she hated children. Maybe she was a child abuser. In the end, they would contend that since it was her karma to suffer it would be pointless to try to extricate herself from her dilemma. The law of sowing and reaping must exact its pound of flesh. But Hannah's victory proved the opposition wrong. It overturned the law of karmic retribution. It pounded fatalism and determinism a devastating blow. Her faith arrested fate and made it conform to her will and desire. It caused good to triumph over evil and it allowed sovereignty to rule. Her victory teaches us that we do not have to resign our lives to fate. It reminds us that we can change our circumstances despite the hand that was dealt us. The idea that some are born losers is a lie. No one is destined for any condition. It would only appear that we way if we succumb to the presupposition that it is our lot in life to remain bound to our circumstances like Nabal in the Old Testament whose name meant fool, and who lived and died like a fool. But no one must surrender to any presuppositions about themselves. No one need to remain in a state of self-abhorrence. Every year we read about people who defied the odds stacked against them in life and prevailed. How much more should not we who know God surmount our obstacles and clear the hurdles in our way. We have been assured that God is on our side, that He will never leave us nor forsake us in our lifetime. He changed the course of Hannah's life, and He can do the same for every one of us who believes He has the power and willingness to transform our lives.

Again, it is important that we understand our faith is not predetermined. Many miserable comforters will try their utmost best to let us believe we have no control over what is happening to us. Others will tell us it is a generational curse. It is in the family. There is nothing we can do about it. Accept your lot and move on. This is essentially what Elkanah was saying to Hannah to bring her comfort. He said he was better to her than ten sons. In other words, he was saying she had no real justifiable reason for being sad. He was saying, look on the bright side. You have some positive things going for you.

Still, others will try to persuade us to believe that somewhere, somehow, we did something to deserve our adversity. But nowhere in the biblical narrative is it said or implied that Hannah's womb was shut because of divine judgment. Peninah assumed it was so and this gave her the gumption to use her fertility to lord it over her rival. Interestingly, the Bible tells us that God opened Leah's (Jacob's first wife) womb because other women ridiculed her (Gen.29: 31). And perhaps it was Peninah's taunts that moved God to open Hannah's womb. The lesson here is that when your enemies taunt and oppress you take your cares to the Lord in prayer. In his arms, he will take and shield you and you will find a solace there.

2: We must be determined to persevere with God if we desire to change our circumstances.

Change will not come accidentally. If we do not persevere, fate will take over. But Hannah and her community were not fated (*WB, p.16*) and she will not allow them to be. Scripture makes at least four references to Hannah's intercession in chapter 1 (vs. 10, 12, 26, 27), with an additional reference in 2:1.

This persevering faith results from seeing God at the center of everything. Brueggemann observed that God stood at the center of every episode in this drama:

1. The Lord had closed her womb (Vv. 5, 6).
2. The God of Israel grants your petition (v. 17).
3. The Lord remembered her (v. 19).
4. The Lord has granted me my petition (v. 27). (*WB, p.15*).

Life has to do with the power and fidelity of God (WB, p.15). He must be seen in all and over all. Without him, we are nothing and can do nothing. In him, we live, and move, and have our being. He is the Vine, and we are the branches. Apart from him, we are dead and fruitless. Hence, anytime we are tempted to act apart from God we will experience barrenness and spiritual death. Perhaps, as the opening narrative of 1 Samuel, this story serves to warn Israel against departing from the government of the living God to be like the other nations. Only barrenness can result from such a course of action.

Strangely it is barrenness that invokes God. When we are in close communion with God there is no barrenness. When we become independent of God barrenness enters and we are forced back to safety in Him. True are the words of St. Augustine that we are restless until we rest in God. Yahweh must be seen as the key player in both individual lives and that of a nation. As Israel's new power would emerge out of their leadership barrenness, so Hannah's "horn" will emerge out of her physical infertility.

A final antitypical note on spiritual barrenness emerges from Elkanah's love for Hannah. Her infertility forces our attention to our Lord Jesus Christ who loves us despite our fruitlessness and reproaches. Elkanah showed more concern for Hannah, even as Christ gives more grace to them that are tempted and faced with greater trials. Peninnah responded by rubbing Hannah's nose in her childlessness on every occasion, hoping no doubt to break her heart and break her marriage to Elkanah and possess him solely for herself. How often do we interface with people who try to break our fellowship with Christ? They fail to realize that nothing shall separate us from the love of Christ.

3: We must pray.

This is perhaps one of the most performed activities in the Church and the individual Christian life but perhaps the one with the least return. This is not to denigrate the power of prayer. Rather, it is a call to the Church to examine why our prayers are not as effective as we expect them to be. How many serious needs have we prayed for and in our hearts are pondering why those petitions were not answered. The Bible tells us that Elijah prayed, and God answered. But James qualifies the prayer of Elijah. It was not a superficial, spasmodic, unfeeling, invalid prayer. Rather it was a passionate and heartfelt prayer rooted in the will and purposes of God for His people. It was not self-serving. It was to restore God to His rightful place among His people.

Hannah prayed and her prayer was answered. And though some have suggested that her prayer was selfish in that she prayed, not for a child, but for a son, it was honored because she vowed to return the child to God. She found an important key to answered prayer. As Bishop Hall explained, "The way to obtain any benefits is to devote it in our hearts to the glory of God when we ask for it." Jesus concurred. He taught us to "seek first the kingdom of God and His righteousness, and all the things we need would be given to us." By this Jesus means that whatever we ask of God must be for the furtherance of His name and His glory. If such is the basis of our requests, we will have whatever we ask for. Hannah was "in bitterness of soul, and prayed to the LORD, and wept bitterly. And she vowed a vow, and said, O LORD of hosts, if you will indeed look on the affliction of your handmaid, and remember me, and not forget me, but will give to me a male child, then I will return him to the LORD all the days of his life, and no razor will come on his head" (1 Samuel 1: 10, 11).

Hannah dedicated her request to the honor and glory of God and His kingdom. Her child will be dedicated to the service of the Lord all the days of his life. This was a dedication of faith. She had no way of knowing that Samuel was going to remain in the house of God and in the service of the kingdom. Yet her prayer intimates that she would see to it that her promise was kept.

The conclusion is indisputable. Many prayers are not answered simply because they are selfish in nature and purpose. We may disguise our intent in pious language, and even deceive ourselves that our motive is right, but God knows the secrets of the heart. He knows when we seek self-aggrandizement rather than the establishment of His kingdom and the praise of His name. When self-serving interests take precedence over the divine will, our prayers stand in jeopardy of being ignored. As Gnana Robinson rightly observes, we seldom find devotion to God that does not expect personal gains (*p. 16*).

Hannah's prayer, which follows the pattern of the Psalms of Distress, contains several elements which we would do well to emulate if we expect our petitions to be heard.

a. Address to God
b. Description of distress
c. Plea for redemption
d. Statement of confidence
e. Confession of sin or innocence
f. Pledge or vow
g. Conclusion

Eli reassured her of his blessing and turned her mood from lament to jubilation. As a result, there is an instructive contrast between the Hannah who, distraught and averse to food, went to pray, and the Hannah who returned to join the family. Though outwardly her circumstances had not changed, she was now joyous and resolute, full of the assurance that her prayer would be answered (*Baldwin, p.52*). This is the attitude of faith with which we must rise from the place of prayer. Faith rests.

The next key is closely linked to effective prayer. We may say it regulates prayer, putting it in proper perspective. This it achieves by reminding us we are temporal stewards of divine gifting.

4: We must remember we are stewards of the blessings of God.

Hannah explained, "For this child, I prayed; and the Lord hath given me my petition which I asked of him: Therefore also I have lent him to the Lord; as long as he lives he shall be lent to the Lord. And he worshipped the Lord there" (1 Samuel 1: 27, 28).

Hannah gave her only son, at that time, to the work of the ministry, clearly understanding that "every good gift and every perfect gift comes from above, from the Father of lights, with whom there is neither variableness nor shadow of turning." And therefore to give back to God that which He had loaned to us in the first place is not that big a sacrifice. Hannah's act of stewardship serves as a strong rebuke to those who have been blessed by the Lord but who hold on to those blessing as though by their own strength and might they have earned it and therefore should decide how it should be employed. Scripture tells us that it is the Lord who gives us the power to get wealth. It is the Lord who sends rain on just and unjust alike. He made all things for His pleasure. Therefore all we have is but loaned goods given to us for the glory of God. When we hold on to them, we will lose them. Jesus said if we save our life, we will lose it. If we save our money, we will lose it. If we save our talents, we will lose it. The man who invested his talents was richer in the end - more talented than before. And an understanding that we are only stewards of the blessings of God should encourage us to put our talents to good and godly use. Hannah gave back Samuel to his

Giver and he rose to be one of the greatest prophets of the OT era, giving us the wonderful books of 1st and 2nd Samuel with all their wonderful tales and inspiring history.

5: We must never forget to express our gratitude to God for His blessings.

As Brueggemann pointed out, "this birth is not wrought by biological manipulation or by dark, mangled religious secrets. It is a pure gift, wrought in the intense conversation of complaint and answer, of promise and fidelity, of need and response" (*p.16*). Therefore God must be praised. Hannah did just that. She "prayed, and said, My heart rejoices in the Lord, my horn is exalted in the Lord: my mouth is enlarged over my enemies; because I rejoice in thy salvation...The adversaries of the Lord shall be broken to pieces; out of heaven shall he thunder upon them: the Lord shall judge the ends of the earth, and he shall give strength to his king, and exalt the horn of his anointed" (1 Samuel 2:1,10).

She named her newborn son, "Samuel," meaning "heard of God," or as some believe, "sent from God." Either translation is a reminder to Hannah that her blessing is from the Lord. Each time she called his name it reminded her of the beneficence and mercifulness of God, and that God is a covenant-keeping, prayer-answering God who exalts the humble. And each time she called his name in a public place, she testified to the grace and goodness of her God and inspired praise and worship in her community of faith. As Brueggemann stated: "God has mobilized awesome life-giving power in the midst of Israel's hopeless deathliness. Israel must sing with Hannah. It is their blessing and hope. But we must be careful to give attention and praise, not to the gift, but to the Giver. Praise is the only speech appropriate to the occasion (*p.16*).

Her song is about a "raised horn," which means visible elevation to worth, dignity, power, prestige, and well-being (*WB, p. 17*). But the "horn" also anticipates the "horn of David," who is the true horn of Israel. It anticipates that Yahweh will reorder social reality, precisely in the interest of those too poor and those too weak to make their own way (*WB, p. 20*). Yahweh is the One with the power to transform situations and the readiness to intervene on behalf of the powerless.

The Song of Hannah

Hannah sings.

Verse 1: My heart, my horn, my mouth, my enemies.

Verse 2: None, none, none - a triad that asserts there is none like Yahweh. He is incomparable.

Verses 3-8: Cases of transformation by the power of Yahweh. The full becomes hungry. The barren becomes fruitful. There is hope. There is a reversal of fortunes. See Hannah switch places with Peninah. God is the one who will turn things around. He established the world on pillars, and He will establish the poor and downtrodden. As WB puts it, "Yahweh's cosmic power is mobilized precisely for the socially marginal. No wonder Hannah sings. The worldly hope of the poor is rooted in the power that holds the world together. No wonder the marginal in Israel joined Hannah in her song! No wonder their songs must be addressed to Yahweh, who is the only one with such sovereign power, the only one attentive to the marginal" (p.20). We watch while the despised ones become the great ones.

This song eventually becomes the song of Mary and the song of the Church (Luke 1:46-55). Luke uses it in the birth narrative of Jesus to portray the radical change that Jesus will effect in the world, and specifically on the fortunes of the poor. 'When people can no longer believe the promises of the rulers of this age when the gifts of well-being are no longer given through established channels, this song vices an alternative to which the desperate faithful cling" (*WB. p.21*). Hannah flings this song buoyantly in the face of the power of death…. Our interpretative responsibility now is to see who can join this dangerous, daring song to this same God who has the power to transform and the willingness to intervene (*WB, p. 20*).

6. We must remember that all we have is made possible by the grace of God.

Peninnah, whose name means "pearl," reminds us of self-sufficiency, that we have the skills, talents, and abilities within ourselves and need to depend on no one.

On the other hand, Hannah's name means "grace," reminding us of the instrument by which we can obtain our desires from the Lord. She reminds us that the throne of grace is accessible to all who will come in faith, with boldness and confidence with our petitions.

7. We must remember the attitude we should adopt towards spiritual barrenness.

Hannah wept and mourned over her barrenness. As saints, we too are called to fruitfulness and if we are fruitless, we need to weep and mourn until our reproach is taken away. Jesus made it clear that "ye have not chosen me, but I have chosen you and ordained you that ye go and bring forth fruit and that your fruit should remain that whatsoever ye ask of the Father in my name He may give it to you" (Jn. 15).

Jesus also said that "every tree that bears no fruit will be hewn down and cast into the fire to be burned." We must not only bear fruit, but we must see to it that the fruit remains in Christ. Hannah brought forth the fruit of her womb and she dedicated that fruit unto the Lord for all his life.

8. We must keep our vows.

It is interesting to note that according to Numbers 3: 6 - 15, a woman's vow could be canceled by her husband. But if he said nothing, or did not oppose the vow, it must be carried through. Hannah had vowed that a razor would not come on the boy's head. This vow corresponds to the descriptions of Nazarites elsewhere in the Old Testament. After Samuel was weaned, Hannah brought him to Eli, the mediator of the blessing. It is also worth noting that pious parents produce pious children. Klein: "What better way to highlight the importance of Samuel than to describe his pious parents, the abuse borne by his mother from her rival wife, her fervent prayers to Yahweh, her piety highlighted against the dark backdrop of Eli's insensitivity, her pregnancy thanks alone to God's remembering her and giving her a child, her faithful and punctilious carrying out of her vow, years after she had prayed" (*WBC, pp.10-11*).

Summary

Hannah reminds us:

- That we do not need to answer our antagonists but silently commit our petitions to the Lord the righteous Judge.
- That if our hearts are pure, our spirits are broken, and we humbly seek the blessing of the Lord, not for selfish purposes, but that the name of the Lord might be glorified, God will answer us.
- To be dutiful in our God-given roles, and to be ever thankful for the blessings of the Lord, keeping in mind that all we have is from the Lord and to be employed in His service - His praise, His glory, and the furtherance of His name.
- That barrenness is a reproach, and so is spiritual barrenness. If you cannot bring forth children for God, it is time to mourn and fast and pray that God might purge and heal you so that you might be fruitful. Samuel, the fruit of her womb, was her reward. Samuel became one of the greatest prophets of all time, and every time his name is called, we will be reminded of his mother. Her fruit was her reward. And when we stand before the Judgment of Christ, our rewards will be based on our fruits. If we have none to show, we will be saved but will suffer loss. Let us be fruitful at all costs.

BIBLIOGRAPHY

Newsome, James D. *1,2 Samuel*. Atlanta: John Knox, 1973.

Baldwin, Joyce G. *1 & 2 Samuel*. Tyndale Old Testament Commentaries. D. J. Wiseman, ed., Downers Grove: InterVarsity, 1988.

Gnana Robinson. *1 & 2 Samuel: Let us Be Like the Nations*. Grand Rapids: Eerdmans, 1993.

Ackroyd, Peter R. *The First Book of Samuel*. Cambridge: University Press, 1971.

Klein, Ralph W. *Word Biblical Commentary. 1 Samuel*. Waco: Word Books, 1983.

Brueggemann, Walter. *First and Second Samuel*. Louisville: John Knox, 1973.

Mary
A Sword Will Pierce Your Soul
Story Text: (Luke 1: 26-35, 37, 38)

And in the sixth month, the angel Gabriel was sent from God unto a city of Galilee, named Nazareth, to a virgin espoused to a man whose name was Joseph, of the house of David; and the virgin's name was Mary. And the angel came in unto her, and said, "Hail, thou that are highly favored, the Lord is with Thee: blessed art thou among women. And when she saw him, she was troubled at his saying, and cast in her mind what manner of salutation this should be. And the angel said unto her, "Fear not, Mary: for thou hast found favor with God. And behold, thou shalt conceive in thy womb and bring forth a son, and shalt call his name Jesus. He shall be great and shall be called the Son of the Highest: and the Lord God shall give unto him the throne of his father David: And he shall reign over the house of Jacob forever, and of his kingdom, there shall be no end." Then said Mary unto the angel, "How shall these things be, seeing I know not a man?" And the angel answered and said unto her, "The Holy Ghost shall come upon thee, and the power of the Highest shall overshadow thee: therefore also that holy thing which shall be born of thee shall be called the Son of God...For with God nothing shall be impossible." And Mary said, "Behold the handmaid of the Lord; be it unto me according to thy word."

Mary is an honorable woman. But she is not honorable because Augustine (one of the early Church fathers) taught that she never committed actual sins because the Pope promulgated the Dogma of The Immaculate Conception in A.D 1854, or because Pope Pius XII declared the Dogma of The Assumption Of Mary in 1950 - that is, that Mary's body did not decompose in the grave but was reconstituted by God to her soul soon after she died. Nor is she honorable because Roman Catholic theologians now openly refer to her as the "Co-creator" and "Co-redemptrix" of humanity. Indeed, millions worship her today because of such ill-conceived and misapplied veneration. The Scriptures make it clear that:

> "All have sinned and fallen short of the glory of God"
> (Rom. 3:23), and: "There is none righteous, no, not
> one" (Psalm. 14:3).

This "all" includes everyone born of flesh and blood, of the human lineage. Mary, like the rest of creation, was "conceived and shaped in iniquity." To infer that it was her purity that qualified her to become the Mother of the Messiah is doctrinally incorrect. It also indicates a misunderstanding of "grace" and "works", and between "Divine favor" and "personal righteousness." God makes it very clear that He is not in the least impressed by our self-righteousness, and through the prophet Isaiah, He tells us why.

> But we are all as an unclean thing, and all our
> righteousness is as filthy rags (Isa.64: 6a).

Someone rightly observed that one might find several uses for rags, but none for filthy rags, except to have them washed and cleansed. This revelation may upset religious people and cause offense to the self-righteous, but the holy, just, and inerrant God handed down His verdict a long time ago. Man's righteousness is unimpressive, inadequate, and worth very little in the sight of God. So, if it was not Mary's morality or personal righteousness that won her the nomination to be the mother of Christ, then what was the reason? We will find the answer in the salutation of the angel who brought the good news to Mary. He said to her: Hail, [*thou that art*] highly favored, the Lord is with thee: blessed art thou among women ...for thou hast found favor with God (vs. 28, 30).

Note that the angel repeated the word "favor" as if to remind Mary of the basis of her selection. It was Divine favor, and not self-righteousness. The angel did not say, "Mary, because of your righteousness and purity you have been chosen to be the mother of Christ." He said, "among all women, you are blessed because God chose you." Some might ask, "If Mary was a "sinful" woman would God still choose her?"

Let me answer by asking a few questions. Did God use Abraham, even though he lied about his wife and, in disobedience to God, fathered a child with his wife's handmaid? Did God use Moses even though he killed an Egyptian? Did God make a mistake when he took "that deceiver Jacob" and made him Israel, a prince with God? Did Jesus consider the personal righteousness of the men he chose for his disciples - among them swearing fishermen and cheating tax collectors? Did God consider the personal righteousness of Saul - the man who "made havoc of the church" - when he chose him to be the "chief of apostles"? The nature of the men and women chosen by God for the execution of His Divine purposes on earth establishes clearly that God's choice is not based on human merit but on Divine favor.

1. God uses modest people.

Isaiah prophesied that the Messiah "shall grow up... like a root out of dry ground" (Isa.53:2), referring in part to the humble environment of a carpenter's home and in part to the insignificance of Nazareth, the place of Jesus' abode. Nazareth is neither mentioned in the history books nor in the Old Testament. When Philip told Nathaniel they had found the Messiah – Jesus of Nazareth, Nathaniel asked, "Can there any good thing come out of Nazareth?" (Jn.1:46). Indeed the Greatest Good came out of Nazareth. The Messiah! And it all began with a modest girl, living in a poor home in an insignificant and proverbially useless village.

There is a vital lesson here for those whose lives and ministries are stymied because they feel limited in what they can do for God. Often such limitation is based upon a misconception concerning their calling and the Caller. There are ministers who are convinced that they can only reach people of their own race or of similar cultural backgrounds. Then there are others who believe they cannot minister effectively to "intelligent" people, and some who feel they cannot reach the rich and famous. They say, "I cannot do this, or I cannot do that, because I don't have the necessary skills or training or ability or equipment." They fail to understand that God has ably equipped us to accomplish all that He requires from us. The apostle Paul boldly declares, "I can do all things through Christ..." (Phil.4:13). It is by the power of the Holy Spirit – and not human energy and learning – that the will of God is accomplished, so that "no flesh should glory in His presence."

> For you see your calling brethren, that not many wise according to the flesh, not many mighty, not many noble, are called. But God has chosen the foolish things of this world to put to shame the wise, and God has chosen the weak things of the world to put to shame the things which are mighty. And the base things of the world, and the things which are despised God has chosen, and the things which are not, to bring to nothing the things that are, that no flesh should glory in His presence (1 Cor.1:26-29 NIV).

The prophet Samuel was shocked when God chose the frail shepherd boy David over his more handsome and powerfully built big brother, Eliab, to be the next king. Then God explained the basis for His choice.

> But the Lord said unto Samuel, Look not on his (Eliab's) countenance, or on the height of his stature; because I have refused him: for the Lord sees not as man sees; for man looks on the outward appearance, but the Lord looks on the heart (1 Sam.16:7).

God uses our talent, but He is not dependent upon it. His purposes will not be frustrated by our lack of ability as much as it is frustrated by our lack of availability. Mary was available and God chose her. And, if you are modest and available to God, ever willing to surrender totally to His will, you too can "do all things through Christ."

2. Living virtuously is not a crime.

Mary lived in a sensuous and godless era. Israel's prophets had ensured obedience to God's laws and now that they were absent from the scene for almost four hundred years, the nation of Israel indulged in all types of corruption. During this time even the Holy City and the sacred temple were corrupted, and the sensuous lifestyle of the ruling Romans only added to the moral decay of the nation. Basically, it was a time when every man did that which was right in his own eyes and where the temptation to sin was so much greater. Undoubtedly, Mary felt that pressure, but she remained pure and undefiled.

We live in similarly confusing times. Today, a heavy price is exacted from those who desire to live unadulterated lives. The young man or woman is teased and poked fun at and made to feel "uncool" if he or she is found to be or confesses to being a virgin. Christians are afraid to confess their faith at their workplaces, schools, and even among friends, for fear of ridicule and rejection. High-ranking men and women keep their faith a "clandestine affair" for fear of being deemed unsophisticated and unsociable. It is a time in which authorities do not advocate abstinence from sin – like pre-marital sex – based on morality but on safe health practices. Yet the same world system that condemns a lifestyle that is in accordance with the Word of God suffers because of that condemnation and is now forced to reconsider Biblical values. Biblical values, alienated from political and social systems are now being reconsidered with the increase in corruption in high places and among high-ranking officials. Americans, for example, are forced to reconsider the issue of virtue. Sadly, they are being taught about virtue by people who have no idea what virtue is and who themselves lack credibility.

For example, Bill Bennett became a millionaire and instant celebrity through his book "The Book of Virtues." Yet, when Newsweek conducted a poll asking, "How would you rate the following as role models for young people today?" Bill Bennett was rated dead last on a list of 9 people. He was given a 25% acceptability rating, below that of President Clinton of the United States of America, who at that time was battling lawsuits that bear on the issues of virtue.

Bill Bennett has a bestseller because of the false pride of humans. If we return to the Bible and live by its precepts, Bennett will be out of business. But because we are too proud to return to the real Book of Virtues – The Bible – we settle for Bill Bennett's inferior substitute. Similarly, we do not want to reconsider prayers in public schools because some bureaucrat is too proud to admit error. So we spend millions of taxpayers' money to find alternative solutions to the problems that would not have happened had we stuck to the old maxim that says, "If it isn't broke, don't fix it."

Newsweek magazine's cover of June 13, 1994, is captioned, "Virtue: The Crusade against America's Moral Decline." In one article Kenneth Woodward asks, "What is Virtue?" He then explains, "It means doing the right thing." Then he cautions us concerning the definition of the right thing. "We live in an age of moral relativism. According to the dominant school of moral philosophy, the skepticism engendered by the Enlightenment has reduced all ideas of right and wrong to matters of personal taste, emotional preference, or cultural choice. Since the truth cannot be known, neither can the good."

Bill Bennett also obviously believes in moral relativism. In his next book, he promises, he'll make "a special effort to find stuff from other cultures." What are these people really telling us? What will they say to Mary if she came to them and said, "Sirs, all my friends are doing it and so I am afraid to let them know I am a virgin. Are my friends wrong not to wait until they get married or am I too naïve?" The virtuecrats would say, "Mary, your friends are not wrong, and neither are you. We live in an age of moral relativism. Right and wrong is a matter of personal choice." My question is, "How can both Mary and her friends be virtuous? Can you see the confusion here? Can you detect a double standard? Moviemaker Spike Lee says, "Do The Right Thing." But what is the right thing? Often, the young man who puts a bullet through the head of an innocent bystander believes that he is doing the right thing. Why put him behind bars? Some people felt they were doing the right thing by enslaving others. Many in South Africa felt that they were doing the right thing by segregating and subduing colored people. Yet, despite its obvious shortcomings, the "virtuecrats" continue to propagate this philosophy. It seems obvious to me that a subtle attempt is being made to set up "parameters of virtue" that will allow anyone to get away with anything. It is easy to see that this is a dumb and dangerous philosophy especially so when the "right thing" is left to be defined by everyone.

The classical and modern-day thinkers list the classical virtues as prudence, justice, fortitude, temperance, faith, hope, and charity, but fail to tell us how to achieve these virtues. However, the Bible does. Therefore, the first step in the crusade against moral decline demands a return to the real book of virtues – The Bible. As we live in accordance with its principles and practices, these fruits of virtue will blossom and grow:

- Fortitude – the strength of mind and courage to persevere in the face of adversity. We can endure all things if we have an abiding faith in an ever-faithful God.
- Temperance – that self-discipline and control over all unruly human passions and appetites. The Bible cautions us to "live in the Spirit" if we desire freedom from the unruly lusts and passions of the flesh. When God's Spirit comes into our lives, we learn temperance. The adulterous woman, the crooked tax collector, the boisterous fisherman, drunkards, and the intemperate, were all transformed after contact with Jesus. Even today, thousands continue to experience complete control over inordinate fleshly desires immediately upon receiving Christ into their hearts.
- Prudence – that practical wisdom and the ability to make the right choice in specific situations. The practice of regular prayer coupled with a diligent study of God's Word will

guarantee prudence. Solomon obtained this wisdom from God and ruled Israel as its wisest King. We are also encouraged to ask God for heavenly wisdom. "If any of you lack wisdom, let him ask of God who gives to all men liberally, and upbraids not; and it shall be given him" (James 1:5)

- Justice – is defined as fairness, honesty, lawfulness, and the ability to keep one's promises. A good place to start is the Bible. Its author is the source of justice. "He is the Rock, His works are perfect, and all His ways are just. A faithful God who does no wrong, upright, and just is He (Deut.32: 4). God is fair, honest, and lawful, and he keeps his promises. His justice is never blind, and His system never fails. "Shall not the Judge of all the earth do right?" (Gen.18:25).

Now we come to the three virtues that Socrates never considered: Faith, hope, and charity (1Cor.13:13).

- Faith – is trust or reliance, but not blind trust or reliance. "Faith is not to be confused with a mere intellectual assent to the doctrinal teachings of Christianity, though that is obviously necessary. It includes a radical and total commitment to Christ as the Lord of one's life" (NIV Compact Dictionary of the Bible). The Word of God generates such faith: "So then faith cometh by hearing, and hearing by the Word of God" (Rom.10:17).
- Hope – is "expectation and confidence." It is a gift of the Holy Spirit (1Cor.13:8), and it motivates purity (1Jn.3:3). King David did not rest his hope in his military skills or in his musical talent or his popularity, but in God. "My hope is in thee" (Ps.39:7, 71:5). Christ and He alone is the hope of glory (Col.1:27) and the hope for redemption of all creation (Rom.8:19).
- Love – the greatest example of selfless and undying love is God. The Father loved us all and gave his Son as a ransom for our redemption (Jn.3:16). The Son loved the Church and gave himself for it (Eph.5:25). And the "love of God is shed into our hearts by the Holy Spirit" (Rom.5:5). To know true

love, therefore, is to know God, and to experience true love is to experience the indwelling presence of Christ in your heart. The world is in desperate need of true love, not the sham offered by the "god of this world." If we all were to experience the love of God, this world would indeed become a loving place.

So then, we conclude that true virtue can only come from an abiding relationship with God, unquestioned obedience to his Word, and complete surrender to His will. Being virtuous has nothing to do with "moral relativism." It is living a life that is acceptable to God, regardless of popular opinion. The majority is not always right. In fact, Jesus infers the destruction of the majority.

> Enter through the narrow gate. For wide is the gate
> and broad is the road that leads to destruction, and
> many enter through it (Mt.7:13).

In matters of virtue and morality, the "right thing" is not what the majority thinks is right but what God says is right. It does not matter how many agree, if something is wrong by God's judgment, then it is wrong. Any attempt to substitute Biblical values for humanist ones owes its origin to the Devil, whom Jesus called "the prince of this world (system)." The apostle Paul also refers to Satan as "the god of this world (system), (Jn.12:31; Jn.14:30; Jn.16:11), the prince of the power of the air, and the spirit that works in the children of disobedience" (Eph.2:2). It may come as a shock to world leaders and great thinkers to know that the real brain behind this world's ideologies and philosophies is in fact the Devil himself. And since he is the arch-enemy of God and all that is good, it follows that adherence to the principles of this world system will lead men and nations away from God. Hence God warns against conformity with those principles.

> And be not conformed to this world: but be ye
> transformed by the renewing of your mind
> (Rom.12:2a).

In fact, God makes it clear that those who live by this world system and by its principles are spiritual adulterers and become His enemies.

> Ye adulterers and adulteresses, know ye not that the friendship with the world (system) is enmity with God? Whoever therefore will be a friend of the world is the enemy of God (James 4:4).

This message is for both unbelievers and believers. God makes it clear to believers that our lives are governed by a new set of rules – Kingdom rules. We are in this world, but we are not of this world; we are not governed by its system of thinking and its principles of morality. The standard of our living is based upon the principles and practices of the Word of God. To the unbelievers, there is also a warning. God is clearly ruling out the "world system" as a viable substitute or an acceptable standard in matters pertaining to life and godliness. To live under its influence is to allow Satan to take control of your life and "steer your vessel." The result is an inevitable shipwreck of the soul. Remember no one must conform to this world's way of thinking or its principles of living. Mary did not. She remained a virgin until marriage. To this day her name is hardly ever mentioned without being honorably prefixed – "The Virgin."

3. We must have faith in God's Word.

The "virgin birth" is a Divine mystery and naturally, Mary was puzzled about this "immaculate conception." She asked the angel, "How shall this be, seeing I know not a man?" (Lk.1:34). The angel gave a brief explanation. The child would be conceived via a miraculous process. A detailed explanation was not deemed necessary and even if God attempted to explain in detail the process by which He accomplished this act it would take a miracle of understanding to grasp His explanation. So, any way you look at it, it is a miracle. However, this miracle would put Mary in a very awkward position. Will anyone believe her story once her pregnancy was visible? How will she explain this pregnancy to her fiancé Joseph? Only the hope and joy that her child will bring to the world alleviated the agony of her dilemma, but that agony was real, and it was accompanied by the frightening possibility of being stoned to death – the Jewish penalty for infidelity (Lev.20:10). Yet she believed God to work things out. She said: Be it unto me according to thy Word (Luke 1:38).

Mary's response reminds us that there will be times in our lives when we will find ourselves in inexplicable circumstances. We will not know whom to talk to about our problems and even if we do have a listener, they might not believe us anyway. You will think about possible explanations for your condition, but none will be forthcoming. You will wander around the house aimlessly, seeking answers but only finding questions. If for you that time is now, what should you do?

First, you must believe that God is in absolute control over every circumstance surrounding your life. Satan could not touch Job's life without obtaining permission first from God. And even then, God gave the Devil certain parameters within which he was allowed to afflict Job. "And the Lord said unto Satan, Behold, all that he hath is in thy power; only upon himself put not forth thine hand" (Job 1:12).

Second, you must take comfort in the fact that the outcome of all your trials and sufferings is always beneficial. "And we know that all things work together for good to them that love God, to them who are the called according to His purpose" (Rom.8:28). The psalmist David patiently endured his trials and experienced the "wealth" those experiences eventually bring. "For thou, O God, hast proved us: thou hast tried us, as silver is tried. You brought us into the net; you laid affliction upon our loins. Thou hast caused men to ride over our heads; we went through fire and through water: but you brought us out into a wealthy place" (Ps.66:10-12).

Third, you must believe that God is faithful and that He will not allow you to be tempted beyond your ability to endure. Nor will your trials last forever. As sure as the sun will rise to dispel the blackness of the night, God will make a way of escape for you – one that you can bear. "There hath no temptation taken you, but such as is common to man: but God is faithful, who will not suffer you to be tempted above that which ye are able; but will with the temptation also make a way of escape, that ye may be able to bear it" (1Cor.10:13). To convince the world that her pregnancy resulted from a supernatural act of God was an impossible task. How could Mary convince anyone of the supernatural nature of her pregnancy, especially when she was already engaged to Joseph? But Mary believed that if God allowed her to get into this inexplicable situation, then He would surely vindicate her obedience to His Divine will. And she was right. God worked it out, as miraculously as He created the baby in her womb. Today, there is not a single reference, in the Bible or the history books, where Mary was reproached for this miraculous pregnancy.

4. We should learn when to speak and when to be still.

Men have always accused women of being too glib with their mouths. I personally believe that all of us are guilty of being too glib at one time or another. There is a time to speak and a time to be quiet. Someone observed that God gave us two ears and one mouth so that we should speak less and listen more. Mary teaches us that there are times when we must patiently "hold our peace." When the shepherds explained their experience of angelic visitation on the night Christ was born, the Scripture noted that "Mary kept all these things and pondered them in her heart" (Luke 2: 19). Again, when Jesus was twelve and was found in the temple conversing with learned doctors, the Bible notes that "his mother kept all these sayings in her heart" (Luke 2:51).

One often feels a compulsion to let out secrets, especially when it is of the magnitude that Mary experienced. Her child was the Messiah whom the world agonizingly awaited. Now, here he was, draped in obscurity, waiting to be revealed. She would recall the words of the angel, the shepherds, Simeon, Anna the prophetess, and Elizabeth her cousin concerning her "special child." But, as she observed the Christ child as he grew up, she saw no noticeable difference between Him and the other children. For a moment, her hopes came alive when at the age of twelve she found Jesus in the temple questioning doctors of the law, but such hope was short-lived, and would remain dead for another eighteen years. During this eighteen-year period Joseph had passed away and Jesus, being the eldest (Mary had other children with Joseph after the birth of Jesus), was most likely the provider, working in His father's carpentry shop. Often Mary must have looked at him "in whom there was no beauty that we should desire him" (Isa.53:2), as he sweated in the workshop and wondered if it was all just a dream. Or maybe it was something spiritual or mystical, beyond her understanding. Nevertheless, the years went by, thirty of them, and Mary saw no visible manifestation of Messiahship.

It is difficult to say what was going through Mary's mind in all those years, but the Holy Spirit, the searcher of men's hearts, revealed to us that Mary kept all these things in her heart. She did not become frustrated, lose patience, or seek answers elsewhere. She did not discuss her problems with her cousin Elizabeth. Unlike Abraham, she did not attempt to hasten the fulfillment of God's promise by taking matters into her own hands. She did not question or press Jesus into revealing himself to the world. Instead, she submitted her anxieties to God in prayer and patiently waited for the fullness of God's time. When we are burdened with anxieties and cares most of us tend to unload our burdens on the backs of others. Some even share their intimate and personal problems with unfamiliar and uninterested people. But if you are in such a dilemma today where you feel that you must tell your problems to someone, then I recommend a Friend in high places. He has broad shoulders, understands the nature of your problem – being tempted in like ways – and wants you to come with confidence and boldness to Him. (Heb.4:15,16) In this respect, nothing is truer than the words of this immortal hymn:

What a friend we have in Jesus
All our sins and griefs to bear
What a privilege to carry
Everything to God in prayer
Oh, what peace we often forfeit
Oh, what needless pain we bear
All because we do not carry
Everything to God in prayer

Godly parents raise godly children. We cannot leave our children to the world system and expect them to lead a life of godliness. The Bible tells us that Satan is the god of this world, the prince of the power of the air, and the spirit that works in people leading them into acts of disobedience (2Cor.4:4).

Satan's objective is the eventual destruction of the human soul. Randall Terry writes, "I believe that there is a devil, and here is Satan's agenda. First, he doesn't want anyone having kids. Secondly, if they do conceive, he wants them killed. If they are not killed through abortion, he wants them neglected or abused, physically, emotionally, and sexually. Barring that, he wants to get them into some godless curriculum or setting, where their minds are filled with pollution."

We should not trust the world system because it belongs to the devil and trust it is to court spiritual suicide. Mary brought up her child in the way of truth and godliness. The Scripture record states that "the child grew, and waxed strong in spirit, filled with wisdom: and the grace of God was upon him" (Luke 2:40), and that "Jesus increased in wisdom and stature, and in favor with God and with man" (Luke 2:52).

Mary did not deviate from the paths of righteousness even though she lost her husband. The pressures of single-motherhood were enough to justify neglect, but not for her. Let us teach our children the precepts and laws of God's Word. And let us train them by our example. Then when our kids grow older, God's Word guarantees us that they will not depart from those teachings (Prov.22:6).

5. Remember to always be thankful.

Seneca said, "Nothing is more honorable than a grateful heart." Mary expressed her gratitude to God. She sang, "My soul doth magnify the Lord" (Luke 1:39-55).

We also have much to be thankful for.

- We must be thankful for God's gift of His Son. Thanks to

God for His unspeakable gift (2Cor.9:15). Have you ever thought of giving away your child? What if it is your only child? And would you still give him if you knew he will suffer and be killed by ungodly men? Now you have a little idea why we must be eternally grateful for Jesus Christ.

- We must be thankful for a heavenly inheritance. Thanks to the Father, who has qualified you to share in the inheritance of the saints in the kingdom of light (Col.1:12, NIV). When we consider that Christ has delivered us from the "kingdom of darkness"; from an eternal Hell, and from eternal separation from God, we should be eternally grateful. One man asked for a "cabin in the corner of glory land." Indeed he deserves nothing more. But Almighty God has prepared mansions for us (Jn.14: 2). He has made us heirs of God and joint-heirs with Christ (Rom.8:17) and has even appointed us to judge angels (1Cor.6:3). Can you believe it? Then give thanks!

- We must be thankful in every situation. In everything give thanks: for this is the will of God in Christ Jesus concerning you (1Thess.5:18).

- We must be thankful in every situation, including adversities, because we know that God is in control and that "all things work together for good to them that love the Lord" (Rom.8:28). Paul and Silas were able to sing songs in the night despite being tortured and fastened in stocks because they knew that when the right time came God would set them free (Acts 16).

- We must be thankful for every blessing. Even if your blessings come through much sacrifice and hard work, the praise still belongs to God. Every good gift and every perfect gift is from above and cometh down from the Father of lights (James 1:17). But thou shall remember the Lord thy God: for it is He that gives thee the power to get wealth (Deut.8:18).

- We must be thankful because we are assured victory in the battles of life. Now thanks to God, who always causes us to triumph in Christ (2Cor.2:14). We are not supposed to "win some, lose some" as many believe. In Christ, we are positioned for continued success.

6. Learn to endure hard times.

Mary never abandoned Jesus. She was with him in His life, in His sufferings, and in His last moments at the Cross. Many mothers would return home bitter and broken after the crucifixion. How could this happen? Was it all just a lie? The angel Gabriel and others told her how special her child was, but no one mentioned suffering and death of untold agony. No one said that her Son would be reviled and mocked and beaten and crucified and categorized with common thieves.

But Mary endured. She wiped away her tears, handed over her doubts and confusion to the outstretched arms of faith, and continued with the disciples. She is last seen praying with them in the Upper Room. On the Day of Pentecost, she too was filled with the Spirit of her Son, and she knew beyond a shadow of a doubt that her son was alive, forevermore.

Many Christians give up on God too soon. We go to Church and are faithful in His service, but the moment adversity strikes we panic and surrender. And far too many miracles are lost in this way. We must learn to patiently endure, and we will reap the rewards. Once when I found myself deeply distressed and discouraged my wife gave me a little plaque for my office. Here are the words:

Don't Quit

When things go wrong, as they sometimes will,
When the road you are trudging seems all uphill,
When the funds are low, and the debts are high,
And you want to smile, but you have to sigh,
Don't quit
When care is pressing you down a bit,
Rest if you must, but don't you quit.

Life is queer with its twists and turns,
As every one of us sometimes learns,
And many a failure turns about,

When he might have won had he stuck it out;
Don't give up though the pace seems slow,
You may succeed with another blow.

Success is failure turned inside out,
The silver tint of the clouds of doubt,
And you can never tell how close you are,
It may be near when it seems so far;
So stick to the fight when you are hardest hit,
It's when things seem worse,
That you must not quit.

Conclusion

Mary is not a great woman because she is the mother of our Lord Jesus Christ. She is great because of her humble submission to the will of God. A will that required an honorable young woman, already engaged to be married, to submit to a mysterious and inexplicable phenomenon of a "virgin" birth, then face the possibility of scorn, dishonor, divorce, and death. Submission to such a request required absolute surrender to the will of God. She must believe that God knew what He was doing and that He would protect her honor and vindicate her faith; that He would not use her and then abandon her. She was not disappointed. God came through for her.

And God will come through for you also if you submit wholeheartedly to His will and purposes for your life. True are the words of this little chorus we sing in Church:

He never failed me yet
He never failed me yet
Jesus Christ never failed me yet
And everywhere I go
I want the world to know
Jesus Christ never failed me yet!

Eve
The First Lady Speaks

Text: Genesis 2:18 & 21-23; 3: 1-7

And the Lord God said, It is not good that the man should be alone; I will make him a helpmeet for him. And the Lord God caused a deep sleep to fall upon Adam, and he slept: and he took one of his ribs and closed the flesh thereof; and the rib, which the Lord God had taken from man, made he a woman, and brought her unto the man. And Adam said, This is now bone of my bones, and flesh of my flesh: she shall be called Woman because she was taken out of Man.

Now the serpent was more subtle than any beast of the field which the Lord God had made. And he said unto the woman, Yea, hath God said, Ye shall not eat of every tree of the garden? And the woman said unto the serpent, We may eat of the fruit of the trees of the garden: but of the fruit of the tree, which is in the midst of the garden, God hath said, Ye shall not eat of it, neither shall ye touch it, lest ye die. And the serpent said unto the woman, Ye shall not surely die: For God doth know that in the day ye eat thereof, then your eyes shall be opened, and ye shall be as gods, knowing good and evil. And when the woman saw that the tree was good for food and that it was pleasant to the eyes, and a tree to be desired to make one wise, she took of the fruit thereof, and did eat, and gave also unto her husband with her; and he did eat. And the eyes of them both were opened, and they knew that they were naked, and they sewed fig leaves together and made themselves aprons.

Eve was unique in many ways. She was the first woman; the first wife; the first mother and the first grandmother. She was also the first story of human tragedy. She was the first sinner, the first person to experience the immense power of sin - its guilt and shame. She was the first woman to suffer the consequences of disobedience to God's commandments - she was banished from the presence of God, condemned to suffer pain in childbirth, and thereafter her desire was to be to her husband who was appointed to rule over her (Genesis 3:16). Later, she became the first mother to experience the sting of death and the victory of the grave when she laid her murdered firstborn son to rest. On the positive side, she was the first person to whom salvation was promised. Her offspring, the "seed of the woman," would "crush the head of the serpent" and free man from the dominion of sin and Satan (Genesis 3:15).

As we consider the temptation and fall of Eve, we are taught many valuable lessons about ourselves, especially our vulnerability to sin, and about Satan, the archenemy of mankind, and the way he operates to alienate us from God. Without a doubt, there is no one more qualified than Eve to instruct us on these matters. She stood on both sides of the fence. She was in Eden, the Paradise of God, a place characterized by peace, harmony, innocence, joy, love, happiness, and face-to-face communion with God. And she was "out" of Eden, where guilt, shame, sorrows, pain, decay, death, and alienation from God was the order of the day. She saw life with God, and life apart from God. She alone, apart from Adam, her husband and accomplice, had the privilege and then the misfortune, of standing on both sides of the flaming sword that guarded the gates of Eden. Hence, she is truly qualified to speak to us about the power and deceitfulness of sin, the subtlety and wiles of Satan, and the vulnerability and innate wickedness of the human heart.

In this discourse, we will look back to Eden, and to Eve, the "mother of all living," and glean some soul-saving truths that will make us wise unto salvation. If we are careful to note and avoid the traps she fell into, we will be able to avoid the penalty of being "driven from the presence of the Lord" on that "great and notable Day".

1. We must flee the place of temptation for prevention is better than cure.

It is very common these days to hear people say, "The Devil made me do it," to excuse themselves from guilt and wrongdoing. But Satan is not to be blamed. All that he really does is provoke the passion that is already kindled in the heart.

> Let no man say when he is tempted, I am tempted of God: for God cannot be tempted with evil, neither tempts He any man: But every man is tempted when he is drawn away of his <u>own</u> lust and enticed. Then when lust hath conceived, it brings forth sin: and sin, when it is finished, brings forth death (James 1:13-15).

Satan is not a mind reader, but he is a keen observer of human action and reaction. When he detects a glimmer of forbidden desire, it is his cue to move in and go to work. He saw Eve's eyes sparkle with desire as she gazed at the forbidden fruit, and that was his cue to proceed. However, he must first test whether his haunch is correct - that there is some unhealthy passion brewing, and this he does by poking in a little suggestion.

> Now the serpent was more subtle than any beast of the field which the Lord God had made. And he said unto the woman, "Yea, hath God said, Ye shall not eat of every tree of the garden? (Genesis 3:1).

But that suggestion must be subtle and gentle. Anything overly enthusiastic would arouse suspicion and discourage further participation. So Satan chose the serpent to execute his malicious designs. The serpent was subtler than the other beasts and would be the ideal instrument for deception. In fact, Satan is still called "that old serpent," depicting his subtlety in deception. He poked in a suggestion, Eve responded, and he was delighted. His hunch was correct. He then prompted Eve to continue the conversation, gradually feeding her passion for power and greatness, at the same time stirring up her rebelliousness against God. Very subtly he changed Eve's perception of God from that of a good person to that of a mean, despotic tyrant. He said: For God doth know that in the day you eat thereof, your eyes shall be opened, and you shall be as gods, knowing good and evil (Genesis 3:5).

Undoubtedly, Eve was fascinated with the serpent and its ability to speak. And she must have surmised that if she went ahead and ate the fruit, this power that set this serpent above the others could be hers as well. I can hear her mumble, "Yea, you are right. So that is what God is up to. I'll show Him." I can also hear Satan's subtle instigation, "That's right. Go ahead and do it! You have nothing to be afraid of," as he hissed and slithered away.

I am reminded of Eve whenever I go shopping. Often, my attention is drawn to some fine piece of merchandise, and I begin to examine the item totally unaware that I am being watched by a salesperson, and sure enough, a little while later I hear the soft, seductive voice of someone whispering behind me, "Nice! Isn't it?" Then the salesperson would engage me in conversation, pointing out the finer aspects of the product. And, not to appear naive I would agree and soon be sucked out of my hard-earned money - the price of false pride.

I have had many such experiences, some embarrassing to share, but I am not alone. Most of us have had experiences that teach us that things are not always what they seem to be. In like manner, Satan embellishes his apples so that they look attractive from the outside, but on the inside, they are full of worms. Many marriages have failed because one partner was tempted into adultery, believing that "stolen waters are sweet," and wanting to test the theory for himself. Many a young graduate wrecked his life in pursuit of money and fame. And many great prospective Christians have backslidden into a life of sin and ungodliness because they were tempted by the "grass is greener outside the Church" lie. Ask the drug addict and the alcoholic if they had any intention of becoming dependent on those substances, and they will say No, of course. If they are honest, they will admit that they were very subtly and gradually lured into dependency. It is with this in mind that the wise man, King Solomon warns against being deceived by the attractive packaging of destructive substances.

> Look not upon the wine when it is red, when it gives
> his color in the cup, when it moves itself aright. At
> last, it bites like a serpent, and stings like an adder
> (Proverbs 23:31-32).

Since prevention is better than cure, it makes good sense for us to avoid the places of temptation if we wish to be spared the consequences of sin. I avoid salespeople because I know how vulnerable I am to their sales pitches. How much more should we not run from Satan, the master deceiver, and the greatest illusionist of all times. The Tempter made Eve see what never existed, and he will do the same to us if we linger too long in the place of temptation. Eve reminds us that when we linger at the place of temptation, we are sure to attract the presence of the Tempter and bring our souls in jeopardy.

2. Every person is subject to temptation - Satan is no respecter of persons.

As a young Christian, I used to think that successful evangelists and preachers were beyond Satanic attacks; that they had graduated to a level of immunity from sin; and that Satan was afraid of them. Years later, as the news of the fall of prominent televangelists was disseminated around the globe, I was awakened to some important truths. Foremost is that no one is exempted from temptation and that even the noblest are in themselves no match for the wily and experienced devil. I also became aware of the fact that Satan never gives up in the battle for a soul. If we continuously defeat an opponent, he eventually backs off for good. But Satan never gives in or gives up. Unlike man, he never throws in the towel. He is a firm believer in the power of evil to seduce any and every man and it is this belief that makes him relentless in the pursuit of his prey. We must understand that Satan is not in the least impressed with our righteousness. He was once called the "son of the morning," a title that depicts true righteousness. Yet, all his righteousness could not stay the rising tide of pride, nor quell the boiling passion for the power that was conceived in his heart. So he was not in the least daunted by the fact that Adam and Eve were sinless creations or that they were forewarned about him in their daily communion with God. In addition, he had already tested his haunch on myriads of good angels, convincing a third portion of them to join him in rebellion against God - a rebellion he knew was futile and nothing short of foolish (Revelation 12:4; Daniel 8:10). Why then should he give up on Adam and Eve who were less than angels in power and wisdom, or on us their children who inherited their sinful nature?

The truth is that no one is beyond the power of temptation, and no one ever becomes immune to sin. In fact, the Bible issues a special warning to him who "thinks he stands" to "take heed lest he falls." Those who are full of confidence in themselves are at greater risk than those who depend daily on the Lord.

Let us then "put on the whole armor of God," and "live in the Spirit," always "watching unto prayer," and seek God daily for protection from evil and for strength to resist temptation when it comes to us.

3. We are more vulnerable to temptation when we are alone.

We understand from the Genesis account of creation that God was satisfied with everything He made (Genesis 1:31), and that He stamped His approval on each aspect of creation with the words, "It is good." The only time God said, "It is not good," was in reference to Adam's loneliness. He said, "It is not good that the man should be alone; I will make him a helpmeet for him" (Genesis 2:18).

Our omniscient Father knows that "two is better than one," not only for reasons of fellowship and companionship but also to minimize the dangers of isolation. It is an indisputable fact that we are weaker when we stand alone, and it is equally true that we are more susceptible to the power of temptation when we stand aloof from others. It is for these reasons that the Apostle Paul - obviously through Divine inspiration since he was never married - advises married couples against prolonged abstinence from each other. He counsels:

> Let the husband render unto the wife due
> benevolence: and likewise also the wife unto the

> husband...Defraud ye not one the other, except it be
> with consent for a time, that ye may give yourselves
> to fasting and prayer; and come together again, that
> Satan tempts you not for your incontinency
> (1Cor.7:3-5).

Satan's first move in the destruction of Eve was to isolate her from her husband - to divide and conquer. He knows that when we are isolated from others, or when we are apart from the fellowship of others, we are more vulnerable to the power of temptation. A couple of cases prove that he continues to employ this strategy to destroy the children of God.

Peter could not understand how his Lord, the powerful Son of God who defied the laws of nature, drove out demons, delivered men and women from every form of sickness and disease, and who proved himself to be "a man of God approved with signs and wonders," could be unjustly condemned to a cruel and criminal death. Totally confused, devastated, and broken-hearted, he disassociated from the other disciples and "followed afar off" (Matthew 26:58). Before the trial of Jesus, he was always in the forefront of the action, always speaking for the others, and always in the "inner circle." But now, for the first time, he was separated from them, and Satan saw an opportunity, and pounced on him, forcing him to swear, curse, and deny having any association with Jesus. Alas, Peter learned that isolation is dangerous. He was later restored but even time and forgiveness did not erase this shameful episode from his mind. Later in his life, he warned the saints concerning Satan's method of attack by recalling his own experience. He informed them that Satan's method of taking prey is like that of a "roaring lion" (1 Peter 5:8). A lion's roar will send a herd of animals running in all different directions. He then isolates one animal and moves in for the kill.

Another example is that of the mighty King David - a "man after God's own heart." Carefully read the narrative that precedes David's fall from grace:

> And it came to pass...at the time when kings go forth
> to battle, that David sent Joab, and his servants with

him, and all Israel; and they destroyed the children of
Ammon and besieged Rabbah. But David tarried still
at Jerusalem (2 Samuel 11:1).

It was a time for battle, and in those days, kings led their armies into
battle. So what was David doing at home? Indeed, he had fought
many battles and could certainly justify taking a day off from the
battle against the Ammonites. Unfortunately for him, Satan
empathizes with no one, and he never leaves us without a watch.
Instead, he looks for and seizes every opportunity to get a foothold
in our lives. By remaining idly at home David gave Satan such an
opportunity. Why was he on his rooftop leering at a naked woman
while his men fought their hearts out in battle? If he was tired, he
should be resting. Alas, many believers continue to fall away
because, like David, they are guilty of deserting "spiritual warfare,"
remaining idle at home while others fight for them. But King David
reminds us that an idle mind is indeed the Devil's workshop. He was
not at his usual place on the frontline of his army but took the night
off, and the rest is history. Bloody and terrible history! Assuredly,
his greatness as a king and a talented musician will always be
remembered. But so also will the defilement of Bathsheba, the
bloody murder of her husband, and the death of his illegitimate
child. And it all began because he was isolated from the army of the
Lord.

It is no secret that temptations become stronger when we are alone at
home, or when we are away from others with whom we are familiar.
We become more vulnerable to sin and unbridled lusts. And it is for
this very reason the writer of the epistle to the Hebrews admonished
the saints to stick together.

And forsake not the assembling of ourselves
together...and so much the more, as you see the Day
approaching (Hebrews 10:25).

That "day" refers to the time of the end, the final days preceding the
return of Jesus Christ for his Church. According to Jesus, in those
days, "iniquity shall abound and the love of many shall wax cold, but
he that endures to the end shall be saved." As believers, we stand a

better chance of finishing the race if we run together instead of running separately. And there is something else we should know. Satan will wait as long as he has to if only to get us alone. Adam and Eve were the only couple on earth, sharing a love that was new and pure. Likely, they were inseparable. And as long as they were together Satan refrained from tempting them. But he never left them without a watch. He knew that a day would come when Eve will be alone and more vulnerable, and then he will strike.

I encourage you therefore to reflect on Eve's fall every time you are tempted to abstain from Church meetings and programs, or when you sit at home in front of your TV set while others are in prayer meetings and fellowship services wrestling against principalities and powers. Remember David and remember Eve. Isolation is an invitation to the Tempter. So, keep always in fellowship with a good company of believers and remember that united you will stand, but divided, it is only a matter of time before you fall.

4. Satan focuses his attack on the weaker vessel.

The apostle Peter, inspired by the Holy Ghost, writes:

> Likewise, ye husbands, dwell with them (your wives) according to knowledge (not in ignorance), giving honor unto the wife, as unto the <u>weaker</u> vessel, and as being heirs together of the grace of life. (1 Peter 3: 7).

I am not qualified to, nor am I going to debate whether women are physically, emotionally, or psychologically weaker than men. But, in the above passage of scripture, God our Creator, declares woman to be the "weaker vessel." And the Scriptures intimate that Satan tempted Eve because she was the weaker vessel; a conclusion he could only have arrived at from observation. The lesson to be concerned with, however, is not the comparative strength of men and women, but the fact that Satan chose the weaker vessel to undermine the plan and purposes of God. And his reasoning is logical and simple. Why break down the door when the window is open?

As a pastor, I am often guilty of neglecting those members who seem less significant to me and to the functioning of the local church. The danger is that these insignificant members are not so insignificant and unnoticeable to Satan. His eyes are on them because they offer him the surest foothold into the Church. We must remember that Satan is a thief (John 10:10), and a thief looks for the easiest way into the house. For this very reason, the apostle Paul warns the Church at Corinth of the dangers of neglecting those "unseemly members" among them.

> Nay, much more those members of the body, which seem to be feebler, are necessary: and those members of the body, which we think to be less honorable, upon these we bestow more abundant honor; and our uncomely parts have more abundant comeliness. For our comely parts have no need: but God hath tempered the body together, having given more abundant honor to that part which lacked: that there should be no schism in the body; but that the members should have the same care one for another (1 Corinthians 12:22-25).

Instead of ignoring those "uncomely members" among us, we should give them special attention for they are the most vulnerable to Satan. It is truly said that the strength of a chain is the strength of its weakest link. Likewise, the strength of the local Church is not measured by the strength of the Church Board or the strength of the membership, or by the charisma of its pastor, but by the strength of its weakest member. And for that reason, we must pay more attention to those weaker vessels, pray more fervently for them, and shepherd them with greater care lest Satan gets a foothold into the Church by means of any of them.

5. The temptation and fall of Eve reveal Satan's model approach to secure the fall of humanity.

> And when the woman saw that the tree was good for food and that it was pleasant to the eyes, and a tree to be desired to make one wise, she took of the fruit

thereof (Genesis 3:6).

In this verse are found the three areas of vulnerability in human nature.

1.   The lust of the flesh   - "good for food"
2.   The lust of the eyes   - "pleasant to the eyes"
3.   The pride of life   - "to make one wise"

Eve was tempted in all three areas, and she failed. By the time Jesus began His earthly ministry, Satan had tested and proven this model repeatedly and was supremely confident that Jesus too will fail the test. So he tempted Jesus in a similar fashion.

Temptation 1: The lust of the flesh:

> If you are the Son of God, command that these stones become bread (Matt.4:3).

Temptation 2: The lust of the eyes:

> Again, the devil takes him up into an exceeding high mountain and shows him all the kingdoms of the world, and the glory of them; and says unto him, All these things will I give thee, if thou will fall down and worship me (Matt.4:8-9).

Temptation 3: The pride of life:

> Then the devil takes him up into the holy city and sets him on a pinnacle of the temple. And says unto him, If thou be the Son of God, cast thyself down: for it is written, He shall give His angels charge concerning thee: and in their hands, they shall bear thee up, lest at any time thou dash thy foot against a stone (Matt.4:5-6).

Jesus won his battle! Eve lost hers. She knew what God said but was made to doubt it. Jesus knew God's Word, and despite the power of the temptation, he believed it and applied it. The Scripture teaches us that the secret to continuous victory is a life lived in active resistance to Satan and total submission to God. Many of course, are unsuccessful in their struggles against sin and Satan because they adhere only to one aspect of this directive. It is not just sufficient to resist the Devil, but we must also live in submission to the Divine will. The difference in results between the temptations of Eve and Jesus is because Eve entertained Satan's offer, discussing it with him, whereas Jesus resisted him quickly and efficiently so that those extremely tempting offers and suggestions were not allowed to conceive. In other words, Jesus aborted those thoughts and suggestions before they were allowed to conceive. And this is the way to deal with temptations. There is a time span between temptation and conception of sin, and it is within that time span those evil thoughts and suggestions must be defied and denied further progression. Like Jesus, let us resist Satan through a determined refusal to fall in love with this "world system," which is characterized by "the lust of the flesh, the lust of the eyes, and the pride of life," and over which Satan is still god.

> Love not the world, neither the things that are in the world. If any man loves the world, the love of the Father is not in him. For all that is in the world, the lust of the flesh, and the lust of the eyes, and the pride of life, is not of the Father, but of the world. And the world passes away, and the lust thereof: but he that doeth the will of God abides forever (1 John 2:15-17).

Indeed, if we become truly involved in fulfilling the will of God for our lives we will have no time for the devil, nor will we have any affection to spare the world. Let us then keep in the mind the approach Satan uses to secure the fall of man and be on the alert. And if we do so we will be able to quench the fiery darts of the enemy before they strike and abort any sinful lusts before they conceive.

6. We must never allow ourselves to suspect Divine goodness.

Whenever we are made to suspect Divine goodness our confidence in God will be shaken and it is only a matter of time before we succumb to a lie from the devil. Satan knows that God is Truth; that He cannot lie; and that His Word is forever settled in heaven. So how does he get men to suspect Divine goodness? He distorts and misapplies the Word of God. In Eve's case, the Devil succeeded in changing the intent and meaning of God's directive. God said to the first couple, "Of every tree of the garden you may freely eat: but of the tree of the knowledge of good and evil, thou shall not eat of it: for in the day that thou eat thereof thou shall surely die" (Genesis 2:16-17). Then came Satan and inquired of Eve, "Yea, hath God said: You shall not eat of every tree of the garden?" Now listen to Eve's reply: "We may of the fruit of the trees of the garden: but of the fruit of the tree, which is in the midst of the garden, God hath said, "ye shall not eat of it, <u>neither shall ye touch it</u>, lest ye die" (Genesis 3:1-3). Did you notice the addition to God's word?

Eve assumed that since eating the fruit was prohibited, so was touching it. But God never placed any prohibition on touching the fruit. To refrain from touching the fruit was the prudent thing to do, but God never prohibited touching it. Very subtly, Satan successfully managed to get Eve to distort the word of God to accommodate the lust that was conceived in her heart.

One surefire way to tell when Satan is around us is when we begin to doubt God's Word. Satan, appearing bewildered, asked Eve, "Yea, hath God said...?" (Genesis 3:1), and by so doing he planted a seed of doubt into her heart. To Jesus, in His wilderness temptation, Satan said, "<u>If</u> you be the Son of God, command that these stones be made bread" (Matthew 4:3), and again, "<u>If</u> you be the Son of God, cast thyself down" (Matthew 4:6). The "ifs" and questions were intended to create doubt and uncertainty in their minds, but with Jesus, the strategy failed. He knew the Word well and applied it effectively.

We too must be skillful in handling the Word of God if we hope to discourage and defeat Satan every time he attacks us. The apostle James advises us to "resist the devil, and he will flee from us" (James 4:7). We resist the enemy, not with guns and bombs, but with the Word of God. We must diligently study the Word of God, and prayerfully apply it in every spiritual battle. It is the sword of the Spirit. It never fails when used correctly.

Matthew Henry comments:

> The devil still draws people into his interest by suggesting to them hard thoughts of God, and false hopes of benefit and advantage by sin. Let us therefore, in opposition to him, always think well of God as the best good, and think ill of sin as the worse of evils: thus let us resist the devil, and he will flee from us.

Had Eve resisted Satan, he would have left her alone. Instead, she tolerated his presence and encouraged him into further conversation, to the point where she was intrigued by his appearance, enchanted with his words, and eventually enveloped by his enchanting proposition. Again, never let Satan get you to suspect Divine goodness. The temptation to doubt God is especially strong when we are faced with trials and adversities, or when we have secret ambitions that we intend to justify. God is a good God, and that goodness is the basis of all His dealings with mankind. To suspect Divine goodness is to make God a liar. And when that happens, our lifeline to God is disconnected, resulting in the wreckage of a human soul.

7. We must guard against besetting sins.

Matthew Henry, the great Bible commentator, observes: "Satan carefully examines each one of us in search for our Achilles heel then he will shoot his arrows at the place of vulnerability. He looks for the weak point, the besetting sin."

We all have a "weak spot", a place of vulnerability - the besetting sin. That besetting sin is a burden that slows us down in our Christian race, and which is responsible for many falling out of the race. Thus, it must be detected and dealt with before it becomes a true "dead weight."

...let us lay aside every weight, and the sin which doth so easily beset us, and let us run with patience the race that is set before us (Hebrews 12:1b).

Some besetting sins include:

- Unbelief: Unbelief limits God. We read that Christ could do no great work in Nazareth because of their unbelief.
- Worldliness: We saw how worldly allurements anchored Lot's wife in Sodom and prevented her escape (Genesis 19:26), and how it kept back a rich young man from discipleship (Matthew 19:22).
- Dissatisfaction: Many are dissatisfied with their calling and abilities, and this delays their progress in ministry and spiritual development. David, the shepherd boy, was delayed when he attempted to put on Saul's armor for his battle with Goliath. Indeed, Saul's armor was more glamorous than David's sling, but it would have guaranteed his demise. Luckily, David recognized that it is not so much one's ability as his "availability" that makes the difference. He availed himself to God and got the job done with his "little, inelegant" talent - a shepherd's sling.
- Discouragement: Discouraged believers hold back the progress of building God's kingdom, such as Nehemiah experienced when discouraged men opposed the building of the wall of Jerusalem (Nehemiah 4:10).
- Domestic Cares: Many converts and potential converts were hindered from following Christ, and many others were kept from an absolute commitment to His cause because of family ties and responsibilities (Lk.9:59; 1Co.7:32).

In Eve's case, the besetting sin was covetousness. She coveted power and wisdom that exceeded that which God possessed. And Satan offered it to her, saying: God knows that the day you eat thereof (from the forbidden tree), then your eyes shall be opened, and you shall be as gods (Genesis 2:5). By saying, "God knows," Satan was accusing God of having unworthy motives. And after planting in Eve's mind that seed of mistrust he explained to Eve why God made the prohibition. God did not want her to be as powerful as He is, and to keep her subdued, He had to "blind her eyes." The irony is that Eve's eyes were as opened as they could ever be, and she and her husband had all the power and dominion they needed to live a happy and totally fulfilled life.

They were perfect creatures.

> And God saw everything that He had made, and behold, it was very good (Genesis 1:31)

They lived in a perfect environment.

> And the Lord God planted a garden eastward in Eden, and there he put the man whom he had formed. And out of the ground made the Lord God to grow every tree that is pleasant to the sight, and good for food; the tree of life also in the midst of the garden (Genesis 2:8-9a).

They had absolute power and dominion over all creation.

> And God blessed them, and God said unto them: Be fruitful and multiply, and replenish the earth, and subdue it: and have dominion over the fish of the sea, and over the fowl of the air, and over every living thing that moves upon the earth (Genesis 1: 28).

They had perfect love.

The *NIV Compact Dictionary of The Bible* (*Zondervan Publishing House*) makes an interesting argument for the love that Adam and Eve shared:

> The way in which Eve was created and the designation "woman" also emphasizes the intimacy, sacredness, and inseparability of the marital state, transcending even the relationship between children and parents (Genesis 2:24) ... Deceived by Satan, she

ate of the fruit. Enamored by his wife, Adam chose to leave God for the one He had given Him (2 Corinthians 11:3; 1Timothy 2:13).

As we can see, God did not withhold anything from them. But Satan made Eve believe that she was denied something; that she was somehow short-changed; that she didn't have it all. When she succumbed to Satan's suggestions and lost it all, only then did she realize that she _did_ have it all. She found out that every promise the devil made to her was a lie; that Satan is a liar and a murderer, without a trace of compassion; that he uses men and women in his war on God and then destroys them in the end.

Satan himself was obsessed with the desire for power and glory. An obsession so strong it polluted his judgment and led him to believe that he could be like God, and possibly even overthrow the Most High One. It was that unbridled lust for power that led to his rebellion and fall (Isaiah 14:12-14). But even though his rebellion was busted, and he learned how futile it is to try to "be like the Most High," he continues to challenge others with the tempting idea of absolute power. "Ye shall be as gods," was the proposition that initiated the fall of the first couple, and it still is the proposition that launches the destruction of countless men and nations. In the Garden of Eden, the supposed instrument of power was the forbidden fruit. Today, it is money, fame, wine, women, and song. Satan continues to dangle these "carrots" before our eyes hoping to make us discontented with our lot but whenever he does let us remember the words of a man who had it all and dumped it all for Christ:

> But godliness with contentment is great gain. For we brought nothing into this world, and it is certain we can carry nothing out. And having food and raiment let us therewith be content (1Timothy 6:6-8)

Eve experiences the costliness of sin.

Sin brings shame.

And the eyes of them both were opened, and they

knew that they were naked, and they sewed fig leaves
together, and made themselves aprons (Genesis 3:7).

Sin brings guilt.

> And they heard the voice of the Lord God walking in
> the garden in the cool of the day: and Adam and his
> wife hid themselves from the presence of the Lord
> amongst the trees of the garden (Genesis 3:8).

Sin brings fear.

> And the Lord God called unto Adam, and said unto
> him, where art thou? And he said, I heard thy voice in
> the garden, and I was afraid because I was naked
> (Genesis 3:10a).

Sin brings about a change in relationships.

> ...and thy desire shall be to thy husband, and he shall
> rule over thee (Genesis 3:16b).

Sin brings suffering.

> And unto the woman he said, I will greatly multiply
> thy sorrow and thy conception; in sorrow thou shall
> bring forth children (Genesis 3:16a).

Sin brings hardship.

> And unto Adam he said, Because thou hast harkened
> unto the voice of thy wife, and hast eaten of the tree,
> of which I commanded thee, saying, Thou shall not
> eat of it: cursed is the ground for thy sake; in sorrow,
> thou shall eat of it all the days of thy life; thorns also
> and thistles shall it bring forth to thee, and thou shall
> eat the herb of the field; in the sweat of thy face shall
> thou eat bread until thou return to the ground
> (Genesis 3:17-19a).

Sin brings death.

> ..for dust thou art, and unto dust shalt thou return (Genesis 3:19b).

Sin shuts us out from the presence of God.

> So He (God) <u>drove</u> out the man, and He placed at the east of the garden of Eden cherubim, and a flaming sword which turned every way, to keep the way of the tree of life (Genesis 3:24).

Can you imagine the shame and embarrassment Eve and Adam suffered as they left Eden while the angels looked on? And can you sense God's indignation at sin and His mistrust for sinners when He closed the gates of Eden to prevent their return?

Without a doubt, there is no costlier practice than sin. One sin of infidelity is all it takes to shipwreck a beautiful home and a lifetime of marital bliss. One sin of grasping for filthy lucre is all it takes to undo years of hard work and sacrifice. One unforgiven sin is all it takes to shut a man out eternally from the presence of God and to demand his extradition to an infernal hell. One sin is all it takes to forfeit your most valuable asset - your indestructible soul.

> For the wages of sin is death (Romans 6: 23).

Therefore, we must not tamper with sin, or tolerate it in any shape or form. Regardless of how it is clothed or how it is termed, or how it may be justified, we must flee from it as Joseph fled from the seductive Mrs. Potiphar. For with a holy God, sin is never justified.

Sin brings blame.

> The woman who you gave to be with me, she gave me of the tree, and I did eat (Genesis 3:12).

Did you notice how Adam referred to his wife when the "blame game" began? She was no longer his wife. She was "the woman." And did you detect the subtle attack on God? Adam in effect said, "She is the woman <u>you</u> gave to me. If <u>you</u> did not make this mistake, I would not have made that mistake." Who said humans have evolved? Eve in turn blames the serpent: "The serpent beguiled me, and I did eat" (Genesis 3:13).

Note that Eve did not confess to being fooled but to being "beguiled." She was smart but the devil was wily. He took truth and turned it into a lie. Like a skilled magician, he beguiled her. Nevertheless, whether we are fooled or beguiled, shifting the blame for our wrongdoing does not excuse us from penalty. On the Day of Judgment every one of us, as free moral agents responsible for our own actions and decisions "shall give an account to God" (Romans 14:12) and be judged according to our deeds.

Our initial response to sin is the temptation to hide sin.

> And they heard the voice of the Lord God walking in the garden in the cool of the day: and Adam and his wife <u>hid</u> themselves from the presence of the Lord God amongst the trees of the garden (Genesis 3:8)

They hid from God and from their own nakedness. They took leaves from trees and made clothing to cover themselves - the beginning of formal religion - hoping to appease the wrath of God.

> And the eyes of them both were opened, and they knew that they were naked, and they sewed fig leaves together and made themselves aprons (Genesis 3:7)

But very soon after they found out they needed to replace the self-made coverings. Over and over they made coverings that would not last. The leaves fell and their nakedness was exposed once again. It matters not how well sin is concealed, it will be exposed and judged.

- Like the sin of Cain it may be done in secret (Ge.4:8-10).

- Like the sin of Esau, it may be done under the impulse of the moment (Ge.25: 32, 33; Heb 12:16, 17).
- Like the sin of Joseph's Brethren, it may be years before its discovery (Ge.42:21).
- Like the sin of Achan, it may be well covered up (Jos.7:21).
- Like the sin of Samson, it may be done reluctantly (Jud.16:16, 17).
- Like the sin of Ahab, it may be prompted by others (1Ki.21:7, 20).
- Like the sin of Belshazzar it may be done under the influence of strong drink (Da.5:1, 2, 27).
- Like the sin of Herod, it may be the result of a foolish promise (Mt.14:6-10).
- Like the sin of Judas, it may have the approval of the authorities (Mk.14:10, 11).
- Like the sin of Pilate, it may be done to gratify the public (Mk.15:15).
- Like the sin of the Jews, it may be done in ignorance (Lk.23:34).

In every case, regardless of the reason for sin, and despite how well executed the crime appeared to be, without fail, sin was caught and punished.

Eve, along with all the above-mentioned people, confirms that it is futile to cover up sin, "for there is nothing covered, that shall not be revealed and hid, that shall not be known" (Matthew 10:26). And not only that but "he that covers his sins shall not prosper but whoso confesses and forsakes them shall have mercy" (Proverbs 28:13). For many, letting go of a sinful way of life might be costly, but remember, it could never be as costly as losing one's soul for all eternity.

God came up with a solution for Eve's transgression.

> Unto Adam also and to his wife did the Lord God
> make coats of skins and clothed them (Genesis 3:21).

And He has a solution for yours. So don't hide it. Confess it to God and He shall have mercy on you.

Eve is made to be a "helpmeet" for Adam.

In the creation of Eve, we see God's original, and still unchanged, design and intent for human relationships.

First, Eve was created to be a <u>suitable</u> helper for Adam.

> And the Lord God said, It is not good that the man should be alone; I will make him a helpmeet for him (a helper suitable for him, NIV) (Genesis 2:18)

God could have made another man for Adam just like Adam, but He did not. Obviously, another man did not fulfill the suitability requirements that God had in mind. Matthew Henry observes: "I will make a help meet for him. A help like him, one of the same nature and the same rank of beings; a help near him, one to cohabit with him, and to always be at hand; a help before him, one that he should look upon with pleasure and delight."

Second, Eve was created to be a sexual partner for Adam.

- For conjugal joys.

> Husbands, love your wives, even as Christ also loved the church and gave Himself for it (Ephesians 5:25)

> Let thy fountain be blessed: and rejoice with the wife of thy youth. Let her be as the loving hind and pleasant roe; let her breasts satisfy thee at all times; and be thou ravished always with her love (Proverbs 5:18-19)

Matthew Henry writes:

> Eve's being made after Adam, and out of him, puts honor upon that sex, as the glory of the man (1

Corinthians 11: 7). If the man is the head, she is the crown, a crown to her husband, a crown of visible creation. The man was dust refined, but the woman was dust double-refined, one further removed from the earth..." That the woman was made of a rib out from the side of Adam; not made from his head to rule over him, nor out of his feet to be trampled upon by him, but out of his side to be equal with him, under his arm to be protected, and near his heart to be beloved.

♦ For reproductive purposes.

So God created man in his own image, in the image of God he created him; male and female created he them. And God blessed them, and God said unto them, Be <u>fruitful</u>, and <u>multiply</u>, and <u>replenish</u> the earth (Genesis 1:27-28a)

Only a male-female relationship can fulfill this mandate. The NIV Bible observes that "without female companionship and a partner in reproduction, the man could not fully realize his humanity."

Third, God intended that marriage should be lasting.

Therefore shall a man leave his father and his mother and shall cleave unto his wife: and they shall be one flesh (Genesis 2:18, 21-24). What therefore God hath joined together, let not man put asunder (Mark 10:9).

Matthew Henry summates: "The bond of marriage is not to be defiled and weakened by having many wives (Malachi 2:15), nor to be broken or cut off by divorce, for any cause but fornication, or voluntary desertion." Yet, today, some people change partners as if they are changing clothes. Even so, we are not surprised. Jesus foretold that in the last days the sacredness of the marriage institution will be defiled by adultery and sexual perversion.

But as the days of Noah were, so shall also the

> coming of the Son of man be. For as in the days that
> were before the flood they were eating and drinking,
> marrying and giving in marriage, until the day that
> Noah entered the ark, and knew not until the flood
> came and took them all away; so shall also the
> coming of the Son of man be (Matthew 24:36-39)

If we truly <u>leave</u> father and mother, put all other relationships in their proper place, and <u>cleave</u> to our wives, to the extent that we are seen as "one flesh", our marriages will stand. This is God's word. Leave and cleave! As with Adam and Eve, all married couples were meant to be together, forever, in sickness and in health, in riches and in poverty, till death do us part. And because marriage is a male-female connection made by God, and what "God hath joined together, let not man put asunder."

Conclusion

The first lady has spoken! Although she lived over six thousand years ago, her words are still current and wholly relevant to us who live in this, possibly the last, generation. And the reason is simple. Sin has not changed; human nature has not changed, and Satan has not changed his strategies for destroying mankind. In summary, Eve reminds us that:

- No one is exempt from temptation.
- Satan never gives up in the battle for a soul.
- We are more vulnerable to temptation when we are alone.
- We must avoid the places of temptation.
- Satan looks for and attacks the weaker vessels among us.
- Satan's model approach is to work through the lust of the flesh, the lust of the eyes, and the pride of life.
- We must never allow ourselves to suspect Divine goodness.
- We must always guard against inherent weaknesses - or "besetting" sins. These provide a foothold for the devil.
- Sin always costs something dear. And if unforgiven it will cost our eternal soul.

- Blaming others for our sin is inexcusable. We are free moral agents responsible and accountable for our actions and choices.
- The marriage institution is sacred, for keeps, and meant to be shared by man and woman alone.

Thus, out of the tragedy of Eden came much good. Every soul that reads about the fall of Adam and Eve and avoids the pitfalls they stumbled into owes them an eternal debt of gratitude. But, you say, if Eve hadn't disobeyed God there would be no need for redemption. Let us not be too hard on Eve. Instead, remember this: Eve was representative woman, meaning, that any woman, put in her place, and faced with the same temptations, would have reacted similarly.

There is no reason to believe that we would have done better than Eve or the highly intelligent angels that fell. Therefore, let us be thankful, not that Eve fell, but that through her the promise of redemption was fulfilled. She waves goodbye to us. But even as she leaves Eden with her head bowed in shame and disgrace, she reminds us that hope for redemption is on the way. The "seed of the woman," her offspring will soon come to "bruise Satan's head" under His feet and set us free.

And, praise God, the "seed of the woman" did come - in the Person of the Lord Jesus Christ. At Calvary's cross, though His heel was bruised, He bruised the head of the serpent and recovered that which was lost by the first Adam. Now, in Jesus, we can live continuously in victory over sin and its author, Satan, "for we are more than conquerors through Him who loved us" (Romans 8:37).

Lot's Wife
A Woman to Remember
Story Text: (Genesis ch.19; Luke 17:32)

And the men said to Lot, "we will destroy this place because the cry of them has become great before the face of the LORD, and the LORD hath sent us to destroy it." And Lot went out, and spoke to his sons in law, who married his daughters, and said, Arise, depart from this place; for the LORD will destroy this city. But he seemed to his sons-in-law as one that mocked. And when the morning arose, then the angels hastened Lot, saying, Arise, take thy wife and thy two daughters, who are here; lest thou be consumed in the iniquity of the city. And while he lingered, the men laid hold upon his hand, and upon the hand of his wife, and upon the hand of his two daughters...and they brought him forth and set him outside of the city.

.......and he said to him, See, I have accepted thee concerning this thing also, that I will not overthrow this city, for which thou hast spoken. Haste thee, escape there; for I cannot do anything till thou hast come there. Therefore the name of the city was called Zoar. The sun had risen upon the earth when Lot entered Zoar. Then the LORD rained upon Sodom and upon Gomorrah brimstone and fire from the LORD out of heaven; And he overthrew those cities, and all the plain, and all the inhabitants of the cities, and that which grew upon the ground. But his wife looked back from behind him, and she became a pillar of salt.

The Bible contains biographical sketches of many women who have made a real difference to their world because of their great faith in God. Notables include Sarah, the wife of Abraham, who through faith "received strength to conceive seed, and was delivered of a child when she was past age because she judged Him faithful who had promised." And Rahab, the harlot, was saved from destruction because by faith she kept the spies sent from Israel. Then there is Deborah, a courageous woman who became Israel's Joan of Arc to rout the enemy and restore freedom, Ruth the Moabitess, Esther who saved her people from destruction, and many more. However, even though all these women are honorable and noteworthy, Jesus did not single out any of them as examples to remember.

On the other hand, there are women of great notoriety, like Delilah, the beautiful Philistine woman who ensnared and captured the heart and soul of strongman Samson, and Jezebel who put to flight the prophet Elijah, one of the mightiest men of God, causing him to request early retirement. Again, Jesus did not single out any of these notorious women as examples to remember.

One may also be tempted to ask why Jesus wanted us to remember Lot's wife and not the man himself. Lot was the husband, the head of his household, a religious man who made a worldly choice that nearly cost him his soul. Indeed, his life story is rich in material on covetousness, selfishness, worldliness, and materialism, and the impact of those vices on the life of a believer. However, in the end, he was saved from destruction. His wife was not. Undoubtedly, it is the way her life ended and the steps leading up to that end that Jesus wants us to keep in remembrance. He asked us to "remember Lot's wife." A nameless woman, whose appearance on the stage of life was brief, almost too short to be noticed, a woman who is so overshadowed by her husband that she is constantly referred to as Lot's wife and never once to by her own name.

Yet, these may well be the very reasons Jesus wants us to keep her in remembrance - it is so easy to ignore the "nameless" and the short-lived, too easy to take them for granted. Indeed, her time was short, but her life message remains timeless. There is a lot to remember about Lot's wife.

1. Remember: Mrs. Lot was lost even though her husband was a righteous man.

Mrs. Lot was lost despite being in the fellowship and company of righteous people. Her husband was a "righteous" man and her uncle-in-law, Abraham, was the "father of faith." Yet, despite the influence of the righteous company, her heart was drawn away and ensnared by the world. Like Eve, she was enticed by the glamour of the world: the lust of the flesh, the lust of the eyes, and the pride of life. Her thoughts were preoccupied with business, with the commerce and industry of Sodom. She wanted her piece of the pie. She saw the iniquity of Sodom and instead of being aggrieved over the sins of the people she socialized with them, joining in their idle and unprofitable conversation, and eventually grew indifferent to the sins of Sodom and became a defender of its lifestyle. She never even objected when Lot offered her virgin daughters to the homosexual gang that attacked his guests. The lesson to be learned here is that being in the company of godly people is no immunity against sin, nor is it any surety of the eternal safety of one's soul. Where salvation is concerned, it is every man for himself. The apostle Paul reminds us that, "every one of us shall give an account of himself to God" (Romans 14:12). And because individual accountability implies individual responsibility, each person will be held solely responsible for his or her actions, decisions, and destiny, regardless of the influences in his or her life. Thus, the prophet Ezekiel warned:

> The soul that sins, it shall die. The son shall not bear
> the iniquity of the father, neither shall the father bear
> the iniquity of the son: the righteousness of the
> righteous shall be upon him, and the wickedness of
> the wicked shall be upon him (Ezekiel 18:20).

Mrs. Lot proves to us that one can be in the household of faith and still be lost. She is a solid reminder to all of us, especially those in the ambiance of religious leaders - like their wives, kids, and relatives and warns them against complacency, of the dangers of trusting in others for their salvation. We must remember that the only assurance of salvation is our personal faith in God. Thank God for righteous influence but remember they cannot save your soul.

2. Remember: Mrs. Lot tried to justify sin.

The apostle Peter informs us that Lot was a man who "vexed his righteous soul" with the unlawful deeds of Sodom day after day. The obvious question is why did he continue to live in daily torment when he did not have to? Lot was a man of means, wealthy enough to make a new start outside of Sodom. I am inclined to believe that each time he bought up the subject of leaving Sodom Mrs. Lot found reasons to justify their stay. Undoubtedly, one of those reasons might be that by remaining in Sodom they could make a difference, but if they left, so will the last hope for Sodom. Another likely excuse is that there are sinners everywhere, but no one must follow their lifestyle. A likely third reason is that since they were influential in the affairs of Sodom - Lot being a local official - they could eventually outlaw all the sinful practices and legalize their beliefs. She may even have argued that it was the will of God that brought them to Sodom and that to leave the city before they see a revival was disobedience to the will of God. That kind of argument would certainly get Lot's interest if nothing else would. However, whatever the reason or reasons, Lot appeared to be a weak man, giving in to reasons that to him were not justifiable. As such, he lived each day in a place he did not want to, with practices he detested, enduring the vexation of the soul and the torment of mind that the spiritually weak must suffer.

In all of this, however, Mrs. Lot must not be excused. She was now flesh of his flesh and bone of his bone, an integral part of his life and being. Together, they had raised a family, built a business, and achieved an enviable social standing in their city. Over the years the two had become one - inseparable so it was not that easy to pull in opposite directions. Considering their circumstances, Mrs. Lot was unconsciously empowered, and she understood fully the extent of that power and used it to her advantage, or, considering her end, her disadvantage. Her subtle plans and plots backfired, and the truth was eventually exposed in her iodized form standing outside of Sodom with her face turned to the place she loved.

She reminds us all, men and women, husbands, and wives, that no one should ever use their power, privilege, or position of influence to advance their own agenda, knowing secretly in their hearts that the motive is fleshly and selfish, and that there is no spiritual profit or advancement to be gained. We as Christians, especially those who are married, need to constantly ask ourselves whether we are being unfair to our partners; whether we have hidden motives for the advice we give each other, or the decisions we make for our family. Are we open and honest with each other? Can we disclose all our business and personal affairs with our spouses without fear of reprisal?

Undoubtedly, Mrs. Lot gave legitimate reasons for their continued residence in Sodom knowing fully well that she was not being truthful. But her heart condemned her. She may have fooled everyone else but not herself. And that is the truth about hypocrisy. We must be true to each other, always remembering that "if our heart condemns us, God is greater than our heart," and that whatever is done in secret will one day be published from the rooftops. Finally, let it be said that there is no justification whatever to remain in the "world" after one has been delivered out from it. Sodom is a type of the world or the "world system" which has been repeatedly condemned by God as sinful and adulterated and to be avoided by the believer.

3. Remember: Mrs. Lot was responsible to others for her actions.

Whether we are conscious of it or not, we influence others through our lives and actions. Mrs. Lot was a world-borderer. She was in the church, but her heart was left in Sodom. Like the Pharisee, she would traverse land and sea to make one proselyte but she herself would not enter wholeheartedly into the kingdom; and like the rich young ruler, she knew all the commandments and laws and would readily entertain a theological discussion, but she herself was not prepared to pay the price - to put theory into practice and become committed to discipleship. And her hypocrisy showed. Her children were not deceived by her duplicitous lifestyle. As soon as they were of age they courted and espoused themselves to unregenerate

Sodomites. They became outwardly what she was inwardly, and they did openly what she did secretly. Later still, after they were delivered from Sodom and taken to Zoar, they concocted a plan to drug and entice their father to have sex with them.

What is it that provokes this kind of behavior in young children? It is the example set by their parents. Lot and his wife tolerated the perverse sexual practices of Sodom and to all appearances accepted it as an alternative lifestyle. They were even willing to give up their virgin daughters to be gang-raped without so much as an afterthought. Why then would these children think it a sin to sleep with their father? As said before, each of us is accountable for our own salvation, but God makes it clear that the "blood" of many will be on our hands. God said to Ezekiel:

> Son of man, I have made thee a watchman unto the house of Israel...When I say unto the wicked, Thou shall surely die; and thou give him not warning, nor speak to warn the wicked from his way, to save his life; the same wicked man shall die in his iniquity, but his blood will I require at his hand (Ezekiel 3:17-18).

God has appointed us as watchmen over our household, and He will require an accounting from us for their souls. According to the apostle Paul, we are "epistles, read and known of all men." How we read is important. Can people by considering our lives be forced to ponder theirs? Can our actions instigate inquiry as to the reason for the hope that is in us? Can people see our good works and connect us to God, giving Him the glory instead of giving it to us? If our children follow in our footsteps, will they be led to Christ? We must live with the consciousness that our lives, our words, and our actions affect others around us. When Captain Achan sinned in taking the spoils of Jericho despite specific orders from God, he forfeited the lives of thirty-six of his men of war, brought untold grief to their families, and crippling discouragement to the rest of the nation. And, of course, he brought death to his wife, children, and innocent animals. Without a doubt, Achan knew what the consequences were if he was discovered with the "accursed thing" in his possession, but he was prepared to take that risk. What he didn't think of was the effect his actions would have on others.

Lot's wife may have felt that she was in no way responsible for the actions of her children. But she was wrong. She did have a responsibility to "train them up in the way they ought to go so that when they were older, they would not depart." Had she fulfilled her maternal obligations her children may not have been lured by the bright lights of Sodom; they may not have been espoused to unsaved men, and they may not have committed incest with their father.

The Bible teaches that we have a responsibility to and for others. We are our brothers' keepers and as such we have an obligation to keep others from stumbling. It is a responsibility for which we will be held accountable on the Day of Judgment. And it is this responsibility and accountability that gives us the right to deal with sin, not only in ourselves but also in the lives of others, for when one member suffers, the whole church suffers.

4. Remember: Mrs. Lot allowed herself to become entangled in the web of worldliness.

Although the Devil and the flesh are veritable enemies, they are easily detected by most of us. But the same cannot be said of the subtle enemy of the soul called 'worldliness.' This latter enemy is the one that takes credit for the fall of Lot's wife. Let us, therefore, take note of its nature and method of attack lest it does us similar harm.

What is the world or worldliness or the world system? How does it operate? And how can I overcome it?

John Wesley gave a concise definition of worldliness. He said, "Anything that cools my love for Christ is the world." However, Thomas Ice and Robert Dean, Jnr. gave a much more informative definition: They conclude that "Worldliness is an organized and attractive system of ideas, concepts, attitudes, and methods which Satan uses to compete with God's concept of how people should live on planet Earth. Satan is the head and controller of this system of thinking. Whenever we think like the world, we are thinking exactly like Satan wants us to" (*A Holy Rebellion, Harvest House Publishers*).

Satan is not discouraged when he loses a sinner to Christ because for him all is not lost - the war for the soul is far from over. If he loses a soul his next strategy is to hinder that soul from making an absolute commitment to Christ. This he does by polluting the believer's faith with a toxic mixture of worldliness and godliness. The result is a believer who has just a form of godliness but who lacks the power thereof.

As far as Satan is concerned, the worldly believer is one of his undercover agents in the church. Through him, Satan has access to the church and can secretly steal, kill, and destroy without detection. And that he does with great success. I know of pastors who insist that the worldly believers are harmless; that they are in the church "just to pay the bills." This is the kind of reasoning in which Satan delights. If we believe lies like this, we are already deceived by Satan. The Bible warns:

> Love not the world, neither the things of the world. If you love the world, the love of the Father is <u>not</u> in you (1 John 2:15).

> Do you not know that friendship with the world is enmity with God? Whoever therefore wants to be a friend of the world makes himself an enemy of God (James 4:4).

These are strong, clear, concise statements that describe the true nature of worldly believers: they are veritable enemies of God, known to Him as spiritual adulterers and adulteresses. And for that reason, God admonishes disassociation from them.

> But know this: that in the last days perilous times shall come. For men shall be lovers of themselves...lovers of pleasure rather than lovers of God, having a form of godliness but denying its

power. And from such people turn away (2 Timothy 3: 1-5).

Worldly believers have done more harm to the church than infidels because they are cloaked in religious garbs and employ the destructive weaponry of half-truths. They agree with Emily Dickinson who recommends that we, "Tell the truth / But tell it slant." They are the tares among the wheat, the goats among the sheep, the wolves in sheep's clothing, and blind leaders of the blind. They live a lie and mislead many innocent souls into perdition. And they will have a greater condemnation on Judgment Day.

Lot's wife was caught up with the "attractive system of ideas, concepts, attitudes, and methods" that governed and shaped life in Sodom. Eventually, her heart was wooed and won by the system. She liked it. To her, it was a better and more exciting life than that of her "righteous" husband. But not to alarm her husband, and not to be called a "worldly woman," she pursued an agenda that outwardly appeased her husband and one that simultaneously allowed her to dabble in the excesses of Sodom. She would go to Church but even during the sermon, her mind would be ensnared by Sodom. She thought about how to make more money, how to win friends and influence people, how to be more popular, how to rise to greater prominence in Sodom, and how to use her religion for worldly advancement. She is not the only person deceived by the power of the world system. There are many, including some famous gospel singers, who have "crossed over" to win the lost to their side. Or so they say. But ask them how many souls they have won to Christ since they "crossed over." How can we win people to Christ by becoming like them? Is it not the change in our lives that testify to the grace and power of God to save? If a gospel singer begins to gyrate in front of thousands of unsaved kids, is there a saving testimony? And if they deliberately leave out the name of Christ in their lyrics, how will the unsaved get saved? Did not Jesus say, "If I am lifted up, I will draw all men to me?"

Who else but the singer is lifted up when Christ is omitted from songs and testimonies? The truth is that there is no justification or any scriptural support for a believer to compromise with the world system. Those who do it do so because they are attracted to this evil world system, its methods, concepts, and ideas. And unless they repent and wholly return to the Lord, their fates will be like that of Lot's wife. Let us briefly consider the effects of worldliness.

Worldliness destroys the influence of the truth.

> He also that received seed among the thorns is he that hears the word: and the cares of this world, and the deceitfulness of riches, choke the word and he becomes unfruitful (Matthew 13:22).

These believers hear the Word in a superficial manner. But soon after, the cares of this world and their delight in riches strangle the Word, making it unfruitful.

Worldliness deludes men into a state of indifference.

> For as in the days before the flood they were eating and drinking, marrying, and giving in marriage, until the day that Noah entered the ark, and knew not until the flood came and took them all away (Matthew 24:38-39).

The people of Lot's day went through their daily chores and routines as though they will live forever. Stupefied by excessive eating and drinking, multiple marriages, and licentious living, they never gave thought to their souls and to the warnings of coming judgment.

A similar moral and spiritual condition existed at the time of the Flood. We are told that Noah built the ark and sounded the warning of coming judgment for one hundred twenty years, but no one paid attention. The people completely ignored him and "knew not until the flood came and took them away." Jesus used that illustration as a parallel to the situation that will exist when He returns the second time. The believer who is found in this state of indifference to the "signs of the times" will undoubtedly be surprised to find the Ark of God has come and gone and they have been left behind.

Worldliness makes earthly possessions supreme.

> He that is unmarried cares for the things that belong
> to the Lord, how he may please the Lord: But he that
> is married cares for the things that are of the world,
> how he may please his wife (1 Corinthians 7:32-33).

In this passage, the apostle Paul observes that the things of this world compete for our time and affection, and if they win, Christ loses. As such the believer needs to avoid the pressures of worldly care at any cost, even to the point of having to remain celibate, so that he or she can be attentive to their spiritual state and unhindered in their service to the Lord.

Worldliness molds the activities and plans of life.

> Wherein in time past you walked according to the
> course of this world, according to the prince of the
> power of the air, the spirit that now works in the
> children of disobedience (Ephesians 2:2).

Before their conversion to Christ, the Ephesians were vile and wicked beyond description. They indulged in sin to its hilt. The sins of deception, immorality, ungodliness, selfishness, violence, and rebellion distinguished the way they traveled. And they walked merrily down that road called, "the course of this world," not caring that the "ends thereof are the ways of death." This is the course the believer must avoid - the mold into which the world pours its devotees.

Worldliness leads to religious apostasy.

> For Demas has forsaken me, having loved this present
> world, and is departed unto Thessalonica (2 Timothy
> 4:10).

At the time he wrote to young Timothy, Paul was in prison and the Church was suffering terrible persecution. It was a tough time to be a Christian, and all those, like Demas, who stood at the border between the world and the Church, beat a hasty retreat to safeguard the body from death.

The Bible warns of a great apostasy just prior to the coming of the Lord; a time in which the love of many shall wax cold. Those whose love will wane are those whose affection is shared with this present world, whose treasures are stored in it, and whose life efforts are invested in it. They will be the first to depart from the faith. How do we detect and avoid the world spirit? This spirit encourages the world to have a little religion and coaxes the church to have a little of the world. It advises worldly leaders to inject into their speeches quotes from the Bible and tells preachers to become more liberal in their theology, to adjust their values to accommodate changing times. The world spirit entices the Church to use the methods, concepts, principles, and ideas of the world to win the world. As a result, tea parties, disco nights, rock and roll bands, and bingo, have now become regular features in many churches.

There is a world's way of reasoning, thinking, and doing things that we must avoid. We are citizens of heaven, governed by the rules of the kingdom of God as declared in the word of God. The world spirit, with all its apparent good intentions, is vehemently opposed to God, and forming any sort of alliance with this system is to adulterate the principles of God's government and this is unacceptable. Listen again to God's word:

> Do you not know that friendship with the world is enmity with God? Whoever therefore wants to be a friend of the world makes himself an enemy of God (James 4:4).

Having then learned how to detect the "world spirit," the next question is: how do we overcome it?

First - We need a renewal of the mind. This renewal demands non-conformity with the "trends" of the world.

> Do not conform any longer to the pattern of this
> world but be transformed by the renewing of your
> mind (Romans 12:1).

It is still amazing to see how much the Christian is influenced by the world - in dress, speech, lifestyle, and in planning programs and activities in the local church. Why, because it is easy to conform to set patterns. On the other hand, there is a price to be paid for non-conformity. Every person who decides to be different faces ridicule, exclusion, and loneliness. Yet, throughout the ages, the men and women who have made a difference in this world were the people who refused to conform. They understood that conformity stifles initiative, kills motivation, and hinders progress.

If everyone conformed to this world there will be little, or no progress made. We must avoid the temptation to use worldly principles, concepts, and ideas in building the kingdom of God, bearing in mind that Satan is the "god of this world" and therefore to use his methodology is counter-productive to the plan and purposes of God. We must wait on the Lord and seek His direction. He is the Owner, Builder, and Preserver of the church, and He does not depend on our ideas or the ideas of the world to further His cause and kingdom.

Second - We need to die to this world system.

> May I never boast except in the cross of our Lord
> Jesus Christ, through which the world has been
> crucified to me, and I to the world (Galatians 6:14).

Dead people cannot respond to anything nor are they affected by anything. Likewise, if we are dead to the world, it means that we will not respond to its seductiveness, nor will we be influenced by its way of thinking or governed by its principles and practices. This is the kind of relationship God wants the believer to maintain with the world.

Jesus, the pattern for all His followers, said His kingdom is not of this world. As such He wanted nothing this world had to offer Him.

And true to His word, He came into this world naked and left it naked. At His crucifixion, the Roman soldiers took His only possession - His garment. And after He had departed to heaven His disciples continued to preach non-conformity to the world. John, the disciple whom Jesus loved, advocated defiance to the world system, almost to an extent of hatred.

> Do not love the world or anything in the world. If anyone loves the world, the love of the Father is not in him. For everything in the world-the cravings of sinful man, the lust of his eyes, and the boasting of what he has and does - comes not from the Father, but from the world. The world and its desires pass away, but the man who does the will of God lives forever (1John 2:15-17).

On worldliness, Findlay says, "He can never believe in it, never take pride in it, nor do homage to it anymore. It is stripped of its glory and robbed of its power to charm or govern him." And William McDonald said, "When a man is saved, the world says goodbye to him, and he says goodbye to the world." And I say, never again the twain should meet!

5. Remember: Mrs. Lot lingered when salvation was offered to her.

When the angelic messengers came for Lot's family, they found a family that was apprehensive about leaving. The angels told them of the coming holocaust and warned them to hasten lest they "be consumed in the iniquity of the city." Yet, in the face of certain coming judgment, they lingered, for they had too many material goods to lose in Sodom. They never for one moment considered the value of their souls and the indescribable suffering in an eternal and infernal hell. They were blinded by the glitter of their golden possessions, the things they had spent their lives, talents, and resources on acquiring. They had grown roots in Sodom so deep that they couldn't easily be plucked out. Their hearts were buried with their treasures in Sodom. It hurt to leave it all behind.

This tragedy serves as a warning to all those who build their lives on the foundation of this world, investing all their God-given resources in things that will not last, and who live apart from God, ignoring His warnings of coming judgment and continuing merrily on the path to destruction. Jesus said:

> As it was in the days of Lot; they did eat, they drank, they bought, they sold, they planted, they built, but the same day that Lot went out of Sodom it rained fire and brimstone from heaven and destroyed them all. Even so, shall it be when the Son of man is revealed (Luke 17:28-30).

The people who lived in the days of Lot and Noah procrastinated and lost their souls. And procrastination continues today to be not only a thief of time but also a robber of souls. Why do people procrastinate in matters of grave importance like the security of their soul? The causes of procrastination are many, including worldly entanglements (Genesis 19:16), family cares (Matthew 8:21), unbelief (Acts 17:32), and personal convenience (Acts 24:25).

When a sinner refuses an offer of salvation it is often because he is sorely entangled in the affairs of this world, or he is restrained by social and family pressures and wants more time to sort out himself. More time! These two words are the passwords to Hell. If God were to permit us to enter Hell's portals and interview the present occupants of that ghastly world and we were to ask them: Did you know you were a sinner in need of Christ as Savior? A good portion would answer, yes. Then if we were to follow up with the question: Why did you refuse Him, an equal number would answer: I did not refuse Him. I only wanted some more time. For them, time was flying by too fast. But now, it stands still, in a place characterized by wailing and gnashing of teeth, torment of memory, physical and spiritual darkness, insatiable thirst, unquenchable fires, worms that refuse to die, and eternal hopelessness. To gamble therefore with fleeting and uncertain time is to gamble with the possibility of eternal loss. There is no greater folly than putting off for tomorrow a decision as important as the salvation of the soul. Alas, for those in Hell, tomorrow never came.

The Bible reminds us: "Today is the day of salvation...now is the acceptable time." We must accept salvation now and not when we feel the need for it. Apart from the danger of an unexpected termination of life, there is also the danger imposed by resistance to the truth, that is, the hardening of the heart. This warning is also for believers. We are strangers and pilgrims who must travel lightly and not allow ourselves to be distracted by the bright lights of this world or be tempted to cast anchor in its polluted waters. We must live conscious of the fact that nothing is worth the death of our eternal souls. If we are rooted in this world, it becomes harder for us to be removed from it. When Jesus calls us to come up and meet Him on His return, we must be loose and ready to gravitate to our Lord without a struggle.

6. Remember: Mrs. Lot looked back to Sodom after her deliverance.

Jesus singled out Lot's wife as a sad memorial of the consequences to those who look back or consider looking back to the "world of sin" from which they are delivered. Here are some reasons why we should never look back.

First - Looking back implies regret.

It implies there was an error in judgment. For example, the Hebrews, after having left Egypt, on more than one occasion expressed regret at having done so. When called upon to eat manna and quail every day, they remembered the "onions, and garlic, and melons" which they left in Egypt. They were out of Egypt, but Egypt was not out of them. Their faces were aimed toward Canaan, but their hearts were turned back to Egypt. It was of no great surprise then that not one of them - save Joshua and Caleb - made it to the Promised Land.

We must understand that when we left the life of sin, we lost nothing of value. Unless we count sadness, sorrow, guilt, fear, torment, heartaches, oppression, hopelessness, and eternal death as something of value. We gained everything. We gained life and that more abundantly. We gained deliverance from the guilt, penalty, and power of sin. We obtained release from the kingdom of darkness and its oppressive, thieving, destructive and murderous ruler. We gained hope and life eternal. There is no justification for regret.

Second - Looking back hinders progress.

It is impossible to maintain forward motion and balance for very long if you are looking back. Even runners are warned to avoid looking back since any slight reduction in pace could result in losing a race.

Third - Looking back is dangerous.

For example, try looking back while driving on the highway at the stated speed limit and see how quickly your vehicle runs out of control. We were created to be creatures of forward motion. We have eyes on the front of our heads, not on the back. Our feet face forward, not backward. Our hands pull forward, not backward. Our knees bend forward, not backward. We were designed for forward motion. To go backward is to defy our natural and physical make-up. The same is true of our spiritual life. We were made to go forward, even if we make mistakes. Most people beat a hasty retreat when plans fail. Like the Hebrews who wanted to return to Egypt because the promise of a better life appeared as elusive as a mirage in the burning desert. But God wants us to go on, to go forwards, even when we make mistakes, for He can take even our mistakes and overrule them around for His glory and for our benefit.

> And we know (from experience) that all things (good and adverse) work together for good to them that love the Lord, to them who are the called according to His purpose (Romans 8:28).

Fourth - Looking back renders us unfit for God's service.

> And Jesus said unto him, "no man, having put his hands to the plow, and looking back, is fit for the kingdom of God" (Luke 9:62).

Fifth - Looking back causes us to lose respect and damages our testimony.

It is interesting to note that Jesus used the illustration of Lot's wife to warn against "looking back." She did not go back to Sodom she only looked back. In other words, Jesus is saying, "Don't even think about it." We must count the cost of following Jesus and having decided to follow Him we should never consider defection. The way God sees it, backsliding is likened to a "dog returning to its vomit and a pig returning to its wallowing in the mire." These comparisons, while disgusting, demonstrate God's abhorrence at the idea of defecting the faith.

Lot's wife looked back in violation of God's command given moments earlier (Genesis 19:17), and she suffered the cost of disobedience. This time the price was her eternal soul. Why did she look back? Why do so many who are saved from sin, delivered from the kingdom of darkness, set free from the guilt and penalty of sin, given exceeding great and precious promises, made heirs of God and partakers of eternal life, turn back to the way that ends in death and destruction of the soul? Mrs. Lot gives us some clues:

- She had great possessions in Sodom and her heart was where her treasures were. Also, some commentators believe she had other daughters in Sodom and wanted to make a last-ditch effort to save them.
- She disbelieved the word of God as spoken by the angel. Had she really believed that the word of the messenger of God was really God's word, she would have obeyed that word. But likely, she saw the messengers as selfish men with something fishy up their sleeves. After all, they looked like ordinary men. Further, as far as she knew, the peace of Sodom was not in any way threatened. She was not aware of any brewing war with the other nations. Where would all this fire and brimstone come from and why? Undoubtedly, she may have thought that the messengers were swindlers using terms like "fire and brimstone" as scare tactics in an attempt to dispossess them of their home and treasures.

The same is still true today. Many people view preachers of righteousness as tricksters and con artists who use frightening terms and fearful phrases to make disciples and extort money. As such, many of them are not received as messengers of God's promises and judgments, but as ordinary men playing on the religious gullibility of others for their own gains. The result of their skepticism is that the message is not taken seriously, with the consequence that thousands of souls slip into perdition.

Do you think that if backsliders really believed that there is a real Hell and Lake of Fire where sinners will suffer indescribable agony for all eternity they will defect from the faith? The truth is that every one of us knows that a day of judgment is coming. If there is one teaching common to all religions, it is the certainty of judgment at the end of life. But we willfully choose to deny and defy our conscience, the teacher that lives inside of us, unaware that on the Day of Judgment our conscience will be our chief accuser.

- She did not see the joy ahead of her but focused on what was being left behind. In this regard, the Bible encourages us to look to Jesus as our example. What was it that kept Jesus going? What gave him the strength to endure the sufferings and shame of the Cross? How was he able to endure the "contradiction of sinners"? The answer: "who for the joy that was set before him endured the cross (Hebrews 12:2).

Jesus looked ahead. He looked forward to being with his Father again (John 17:5). He looked forward to sending the Comforter to the Church (John 16:7). He looked forward to the day when He would "sit at the right hand of God and make intercession for us" (Hebrews 7:25). He looked forward to "bringing many sons to glory" (Hebrews 2:10) He looked forward to the time when "he might show the exceeding riches of his grace in his kindness to us" (Ephesians 2:7). These were some of the joys that Jesus focused on, and which helped him to maintain course through the stormy waters that led to the Cross.

We too will experience the "shame of the cross" and the "contradiction of sinners" as we journey on to the end of our race.

But we too have joys to look forward to. The hope of eternal life awaits each redeemed soul. To live forever in a place where there is no sin, no sorrow, no sickness, no parting, no death, no defilement, and no darkness, is a welcome relief after these years of suffering in sin. Yet the absence of sin in Heaven is only half the reason for rejoicing. Heaven is a place of indescribable beauty. The apostle Paul, himself having a glimpse of Heaven, quotes the prophet Isaiah: "Eye hath not seen, nor ear heard, neither have entered into the heart of man, the things which God hath prepared for them that love him" (1Corinthians 2:9; Isaiah 64:4).

As we keep focused on these things that are prepared for us, we will lose the desire for worldly things. So let us put our hands on the plow and look ahead to the eternal joys that await us.

<blockquote>
When you put your hands to the plow
Don't look back
When you make that final bow
Don't look back
And when you hear the angels sing, Allelujah
Don't look back
- Fireworks
</blockquote>

Conclusion

Many Christians look back to the world of sin with a secret longing to return there, but it is my prayer that the Christian who is tempted by the pleasures of "Sodom" would have his eyes opened to the reality of sin and the consequences of returning to vomit" and "wallowing" in the mire.

Mrs. Lot must have been a good woman with godly desires to woo and win the righteous Lot for her life companion. She was also an ambitious wife and an astute businesswoman who, unfortunately, lost focus on what was important and settled for that which was temporary and unsatisfying, using her talents and energies to build a thriving business in an ill-fated city. In the process she became enmeshed and entangled in the affairs of Sodom, always finding reasons to justify her family's stay in the city, to the point where worldliness and materialistic desires so consumed her desire for God that she was totally indifferent to the threat of coming judgment.

Her heart and soul were so deeply buried in the pleasures of sin and worldliness that even the angels had a difficult time getting her out of the doomed city. The sad part of it all is that she was not in the least unsettled about her decision. There is no indication of remorse or regret at having made a mistake. She had to be dragged out of the city like a spoilt child who hollered and cried when it was time to leave his friends and go home. And even on her way out she was defiant, refusing to believe the word of God. Her end was sad. She did not even have the honor of a decent burial but was instead immortalized in salt as "the woman who looked back." The greatest good that can be salvaged from this tragedy is the lessons we are taught concerning the power of worldliness - turning good people bad without them ever knowing it. Jesus asked us to keep her in remembrance.

Whenever we are tempted to trust in others for our salvation, we must remember Lot's wife. Whenever we attempt to justify a compromise with the world system, we must remember the end of Lot's wife. Whenever we are emboldened to act recklessly with our souls, believing that our actions have no effect on others, we must remember Lot's wife. Whenever God calls us to salvation from wrath to come and we are tempted to linger for a little while more, we must remember Lot's wife. And whenever we are tempted to go back or even look back to the life of sin and the kingdom of darkness from which we have been delivered, let us remember Lot's wife.

If we keep her in continuous remembrance, we will avoid the mistakes she made and be spared the fate she was condemned to suffer. *"Remember Lot's wife!"*

The Syro-Phoenician Woman
Story Text: Matthew 15:21-28

Then went Jesus thence and departed into the coasts of Tyre and Sidon. And behold, a woman of Canaan came out of the same coasts, and cried unto him, saying, Have mercy on me, O Lord, thou son of David; my daughter is grievously vexed with a devil. But he answered her not a word. And his disciples came and besought him, saying, Send her away; for she cries after us. But he answered and said, I am not sent but unto the lost sheep of the house of Israel. Then came she and worshipped him, saying, Lord, help me. But He answered and said, "It is not meet to take the children's bread and cast it to dogs." And she said, "Truth, Lord: yet the dogs eat of the crumbs that fall from their masters' table." Then Jesus answered and said unto her, "O woman, great is thy faith. Be it unto thee even as thou wilt." And her daughter was made whole from that very hour.

The writer of the letter to the Hebrews informs us that faith is an indispensable element in establishing and maintaining a relationship with God.

> But without faith it is impossible to please Him
> (God): for he that cometh to God must believe that He
> is and that He is a rewarder of them that diligently
> seek Him (Heb.11:6).

We know that it requires faith, not empirical evidence, to accept the existence of God. And that it takes faith, not works of righteousness we have done, to please God. And it demands faith, not logic, to believe that God rewards those who live for Him.

The Syro-Phoenician woman (also referred to as the Canaanite woman) had the faith to believe that God could deliver her daughter from demon possession. Jesus was impressed and publicly commended her faith, saying, "O woman, great is thy faith" (v.28).

In this discourse, I will suggest a few reasons for this Divine commendation of faith with the intent that you too can develop like faith and obtain the desires of your heart.

These reasons are discussed under two main headings:

1. Her perception of God
2. Her persistence with God

I: Her perception of God.

It is vitally important for us to have a proper understanding of who God is and what His will is for us. The fact that very few people in our society today have faith in God is partly attributable to numerous misconceptions that pervade the religious world - especially non-Biblical faiths and religions. Let us examine some prevalent misconceptions about God.

Different perceptions of God

- The Christian Science movement teaches that God is "all-in-all, the only intelligence of the universe, including man."
- Spiritualism teaches that "God is without shape and form and is impersonal. The spark of Divinity dwells in all."
- Jehovah's Witnesses teach that "Jesus Christ is not one God with the Father and that the Holy Spirit is God's Active Force, not a person."
- Armstrongism teaches that "God is a Family, a Kingdom, not a limited trinity." They say that "God is reproducing Himself and man was created to literally become God."
- The Mormons say that God "is a progressive being who possesses the capacity of eternal increase. Perhaps He was once a child and mortal like ourselves."
- Eastern Mysticism teaches that God "is all there is. All visible objects are but modifications of his self-existence, of an unconscious and impersonal presence which is called God."
- The Unity Movement teaches that "God is not a person

having life, intelligence, love, and power."

- The Unification Church teaches that "God, being the First Cause of all creation, also exists because of the reciprocal relationship between the dual characteristics of positivity and negativity. They call the positivity and negativity of God, "masculinity" and "femininity," respectively.
- Buddhism teaches that "there is no absolute God" The Buddha did not deny the existence of God outright but said that the question of His existence tends not to edification. That is, those seeking enlightenment need to concentrate on their own spiritual paths themselves rather than relying on outside support.
- Hinduism has many gods or incarnations of gods. All are seen as manifestations of the one Supreme Being, Brahman, who is described as impersonal and uninvolved with life on earth.
- Islam teaches that justice is Allah's most important feature. His purposes are always serious. God is a far-away, unreachable, and incomprehensible being who wants to be left alone, a "sword of Damocles" hanging over the heads of potential miscreants.
- Judaism teaches that "God has a certain remoteness...and His ways are inscrutable to man."

And while the list goes on and on, the confusion among them is obvious. If God is impersonal, what sense is there in trying to establish a personal relationship with him? If I am divine, why do I need God? If Jesus Christ is not Divine and equal with the Father, then why should I trust Him to deliver me from sin and make me acceptable with the Father? If God is mortal and limited like me, why should I trust him for eternal life? If God does not have life, intelligence, love, and power, what is His relevance to the Unitarians? The point is clear: Man has a poor perception of God, and unless corrected, he cannot establish a meaningful relationship with his Creator.

Part of the reason for Christ's commendation of this Canaanite woman's faith is because she, an unlearned "heathen", had a perfectly accurate and Biblical perception of God, unlike the Pharisees, the Scribes, and the religious Jews, even though they were exposed to the Scriptures.

She perceived that God is impartial.

Since this woman was a Canaanite, it meant that she did not belong to the "House of Israel", the chosen people of God. To the Jewish people, the Gentiles were untouchables, barbaric in behavior, and totally dispensable. In fact, Jesus tested the durability of this woman's faith by referring to her nation as "dogs" - the term used by Jews in those days to refer to Gentile nations. Jesus said to her, "It is not meet to take the children's (Jews) bread and cast it to dogs (Gentiles)" (v.26).

It is interesting to note that even after Jesus departed from this world the Jewish Christians continued to believe that they were a racially and spiritually superior people. Peter, the Jewish leader of the apostles was reluctant to preach the gospel to the Gentiles. Later he was astonished at the outpouring of God's Spirit in Cornelius' (a Gentile) home.

> Then Peter opened his mouth, and said, Of a truth, I perceive that God is no respecter of persons: but in every nation he that fears Him, and works righteousness, is accepted with Him (Acts 10: 34, 35).

It took the experience at Cornelius' home to make Peter understand that God is not a respecter of persons, or of races, or of cultures, or the social, economic, and religious standing of peoples and societies. The Canaanite woman was neither an apostle nor an inner circle disciple like Peter. She did not have access to the spiritual resources available to the Jews, but her conceptual understanding of God exceeded that of Peter. As far as she was concerned, anyone who claims to be God must be a just person, and if He is just then His requirements must be the same for all men since He must treat all men equally, both in rewards and in judgments. Therefore, this man Jesus, the Son of God, who claims equality with God, will do for her what He has done for others.

Such faith astonishes even the Son of God, for it is a faith that transcends racial, social, cultural, and intellectual boundaries. It is a faith that does not reduce God to a white or black person; it does not embarrass God by associating Him only with one group; it does not devalue God by bringing Him down to the realm of men. It is a faith that understands that God is not a ballplayer going to the highest bidder, but rather He comes to all men on the same terms.

Those who are special to God are not people who think themselves special because of a sovereign act of God but are people who love Him and do His will. God once chose a donkey to speak to a wayward prophet, but that sovereign act of God did not make the donkey any more special than the other donkeys. That donkey was available at the time and God chose him for His purposes. That choice was not, and never will be, based on merit. Isaiah tells us why.

> For all our righteousness are as filthy rags (Isa.64:6).

Therefore, when you come to God, you must understand that in God's eyes you are equal to any other person in this world. God will not withhold anything from you because of your color, race, sex, or culture. If anything is denied you, it is denied you because of your own misconception of God.

She perceived God as a merciful being.

> She said to Jesus, "Have <u>mercy</u> on me, O Lord"
> (v.22).

God did not become merciful because man fell helplessly into sin, or because lost mankind was consigned to eternal separation from Him and bound for eternal death in a burning Hell. Neither was the attribute of mercy developed by God in response to man's need for forgiveness and redemption. God was, is, and will always be merciful because it is His eternal nature.

> The mercy of the Lord is from everlasting to
> everlasting (Psalm 103:17).

The Bible also declares that the extent of God's mercy is boundless.

> For thy mercy is great above the heavens (Psalm 108:4).

Thus, there is none who have fallen so deep to be beyond the mercy of God. The apostle Paul, one of the greatest missionaries and apologists of the faith attributed his transformation from "the chief of sinners" to the "chief of apostles," to the boundless mercy of God. And God's great mercy is the basis for the confidence and boldness we have when we approach the throne of God in time of need.

> Let us, therefore, come boldly unto the throne of
> grace that we may obtain mercy, and find grace to
> help in time of need. (Heb.4:16).

The Canaanite woman was confident in her approach because she knew that God was "plenteous of mercy", willing, able, and ready to meet her needs.

She perceived God as unlimited in power.

Parents, here are a few questions for you. Have you ever had a child who was sick? If so, what did you do to ensure that your child's health would be restored? Naturally, you took that child to the doctor, right? But if you showed up at the doctor's office without the child you will be considered crazy, and he might be tempted to refer you to a psychiatrist.

This woman did not take the sick child with her, and it was not an accident. It was intentional, but not presumptuously so. Her decision to leave the child at home was based on a phenomenal perception of the power of God. How phenomenal? Consider believers in the Church today. Many Christians do not believe that God is able to heal them unless they are "seen and touched" by the pastor or the elders of the church. Like Naaman the Syrian they believe that the "man of God must come out to me, and stand, and call on the name of the Lord his God, and strike his hand over the place, and recover the leper" (2 Kings.5:11). This woman, however, perceived that God is not limited by distance. Like the Roman centurion who said, "Speak the words and make my servant whole," she knew God has only to speak the word to make her child well again. She was not of the "household of faith," yet her faith in God's power exceeded that of most believers today. She believed that when the Son of God spoke the words of deliverance, God's restorative and creative powers will respond to produce the desired effect, regardless of distance or realm. And she was right. As Jesus spoke, His words penetrated the realms of darkness, from where He was to where this woman lived and evicted the demon from the child. Her daughter was made whole from that very hour (v.28).

Let us, therefore, glean from this that God's healing powers are not restricted to the church altar or to a special place. A simple prayer of faith can reach you anywhere and make you whole.

She perceived God as a willing deliverer.

Some people who believe in God do not question His ability to heal, but they question His willingness to heal. Is God willing to heal us when we are sick? Can we really trust Him to deliver our loved ones from sicknesses, diseases, and demons?

Many Bible scholars and notable preachers would answer in the affirmative. Others will say, emphatically, no. Some say that healings do not take place; some say healings are staged, and some say that healings are illusions of the mind. Fortunately, Jesus does not share their views.

Hugh Jeter observes that only <u>once</u> in the New Testament do we find anyone who questioned the will of Christ to heal. It was an outcast leper. He came to Jesus and said, "Lord, if thou wilt, thou canst make me clean." And Jesus put forth His hand and touched him and said, "<u>I will</u>; be thou clean" (Mt.8:3). Jeter then explains, in his book, *By His Stripes, Gospel Publishing House, 1977*) why God wills to heal.

Christ came to do the Father's will and healed all who came to him

> For I came down from heaven, not to do mine own
> will, but the will of Him that sent me (John 6:38).

That will include healing and whom did He heal?

> When the even was come, they brought many that
> were possessed with devils: and He cast out the spirits
> with His Word, and He healed all that were sick
> (Mt.8:16).
> But when Jesus knew it, He withdrew Himself from
> thence: and great multitudes followed Him, and He
> healed them all (Mt.12:15).

Christ came to destroy the works of the devil. This includes sin and sickness

> For this purpose the Son of God was manifested, that
> He might destroy the works of the devil (1 John 3:8).
>
> How God anointed Jesus of Nazareth with the Holy
> Ghost and with power: who went about doing good
> and healing all who were oppressed of the devil; for
> God was with Him (Acts 10:38).

Christ Said it was His will to heal everyone. There is no favoritism with God.

> Of a truth I perceive that God is no respecter of persons (Acts
> 10:38).

As a merciful Father, God wants to give good things to His children.

> If you then, being evil, know how to give good gifts
> unto your children, how much more shall your Father
> who is in heaven give good things to them that ask
> Him? (Mt.7:11).

He had revealed Himself to us as our healer.

> I am the Lord that heals thee (Ex.15:26).

Jeter notes that the tense used is the last clause in the present and can be translated: "I the Lord am healing thee."

He bore our sicknesses; therefore we do not have to bear them.

> By whose (Jesus) stripes, you <u>were</u> healed (1 Peter 2:24).

> Jesus Christ is the same yesterday, today, and forever (Heb.13:8).

Jeter notes that God is perfect and that any change from perfection would have to be imperfection, and this is why God is immutable, or unchanging. He concludes: "On the basis of the above facts, I feel that the following statement is a safe assumption: So far as the ultimate will of God is concerned, it may be maintained that it is always His will to heal, and the request for healing and the exercise of faith is always in order."

Those who spend endless hours attempting to refute and deny every reported case of divine healing will find themselves on a veritable impossible mission. They might do well to consider the basis of this woman's faith. It was not based upon the outcome of theological arguments for and against divine healing, but upon the power, goodness, and mercy of an unchanging God. It was a faith that understood that mercy is not static and theoretical, but like love, it is dynamic and demonstrative. God has not changed, and He never will (Mal. 3:6), and if His mercy was demonstrated in times past in acts of deliverance, it will be manifested today and tomorrow in a similar fashion. This woman found the first key to deliverance, - a firm belief in God's will to heal the sick and save the lost.

II: Her Persistence with God.

   a.   She persisted against family restraints.

The fact that no mention is made of a husband, or any family member indicates that this woman's decision to go to Christ was probably not a popular one. It is possible that she went despite restraints by other family members. I believe they told her that her trip was going to be futile and wasteful. I believe they reminded her that she was a Gentile and "outside of the House of Israel". I believe they discouraged her even as she packed and left. But she persevered. She had her mind made up and nothing was going to stop her mission of faith, not even her family. She must have been conscious of the truth the prophet Micah learned from experience, that, "a man's enemies are they of his own household" (Micah 7:6).

Most new converts I know who have faced persecution and discouragement did so from family members. I recall a young man who immediately after he became a Christian was confronted with all forms of opposition, at home and by friends. He was told that he already had a religion, and he would be ostracized from home and community if he persisted with "those Christian people." Fearful, he backslid into a life of sin that made his former way of life seem venerable. But this woman refused to retreat or recant. She stood firm in her resolve to get to Christ, even though no one supported her. She must have reasoned that she had nothing to lose anyway.

b.   She persisted against the "church people."

Now here is something shameful. To get to Christ this woman had to prevail against the Church. She was "crying after" the disciples, most likely to obtain reinforcement for her cause. But instead of asking Jesus to help this woman who had come from afar and had shown great faith and courage, they asked Jesus to send her away. To the disciples, she was an embarrassment and an unnecessary bother. What a shame!

It is a shame that we must warn young converts about hypocrisy in the church. It is a bigger shame that we must discriminate between churches when we recommend converts for fellowship. The sad truth is that we have to because the church is still congested with hypocrites, and they are the ones who drive away many prospective converts from Christ. They form a hedge around Christ. They are the exclusive insiders, God's chosen elect. Or so they think. In this woman's case, the members were all Jewish.

Today, different churches form different hedges. Some barricade themselves from different races; some barricade themselves from poor people, and some barricade themselves from uneducated people. One sister said to me, "Well I go to the big-shot church down the block, and they don't talk to me. But it doesn't bother me. I go to pray to God and listen to His word." That, indeed, is a noble approach to serving Christ but the local church is not justified in practicing isolationist policies. God is angry when the Church demarcates boundaries for acceptance. The only requirement He gave for acceptance in the Church is to "repent of your sins, accept Christ as Savior and confess Him as Lord."

Church leaders who persist - whether secretly or openly - to practice isolationist policies may do well to remember the story of the black man who stood outside the doors of a church with a white congregation because he was not allowed to enter. As he stood outside and prayed, Jesus quietly appeared and stood beside him. He asked the man, "Why are you standing outside?" The man answered, "Lord, they will not allow me in." Jesus then replied, "They will not allow me in either."

So, when you come to Christ, expect opposition and occasional persecution. Hypocrites and sincerely mistaken people will always be in the church, but on the Day of Judgment, the "sheep" will be separated from the "wolves," and the "tares" from the "wheat." They will be exposed, to the wonderment of many, and then be judged. So "let your courage rise with danger, and strength to strength oppose."

    c.   She persisted despite delay and discouragement.

While we do not know how much time elapsed from the time this woman arrived at the scene to the time her request was granted, we do know that it was more than a day. Remember, she traveled along the coasts, and she was "pushed around" in the true sense of the term. She went first to Jesus and then from disciple to disciple, and back to Jesus. Many potential "miracle seekers" would give up by this time and go home, but not this woman. Delay was not denial. She could wait. And wait she did.

As humans, we are creatures of little patience. God on the other hand has a lot of patience and He wants to develop in each of us this important and eternal grace. In fact, God saw it necessary to teach it to His own blessed Son.

> For it became him, for whom are all things and by whom are all things, in bringing many sons unto glory to make the Captain of their salvation perfect through sufferings (Heb. 2:10).

There is no substitute for patience. I used to think that if I had real faith in God my prayers would be answered instantly. I have since learned that faith is not a substitute for patience. Even Abraham, the father of faith had to learn patience. "And so, after he had patiently endured, he obtained the promise (the child)" (Heb. 6:15).

Why is it so necessary for God to develop the character trait of patience? The Bible gives a few reasons.

i. Patience results in true happiness.

> Behold, we count them happy which endure. Ye have heard of the patience of Job and have seen the end (James 5:11).

ii. Patience is an attribute of true faith.

> We glory in you...for your patience and faith in all your persecutions and tribulations that you endure: which is a manifest token of the righteous judgment of God, that you may be counted worthy of the kingdom of God, for which you also suffer (2 Th.1:4-5).

iii. Patience produces completeness of character.

But let patience have her perfect work, that you may
be perfect and entire, wanting nothing (James 1:4).

iv.   Patience is essential to reward.

Be patient therefore, brethren, unto the coming of the
Lord. Behold, the husbandman waits for the precious
fruit of the earth, and hath long patience for it, until
he receives the early and latter rain (James 5:7).

The Canaanite woman was not discouraged by delay. She recognized
that "delay is never denial, but infinite love and wisdom, planning an
answer bigger than our biggest asking." She patiently persevered and
obtained her desire.

v.   She persisted against apparent denial.

Note Jesus' response to her initial cry for help: "But He (Jesus)
answered her not a word." Jesus ignored her and she then turned to
His disciples for help. But, instead of helping her, they beseeched
Jesus to chase her away. Undaunted, she returned to Jesus, only to
get from Him a response that appeared even worse than the first: "It
is not meet for me to take the children's bread and cast it to dogs
(v.26).

At this stage most of us will give up and go away, mumbling
obscenities and blasphemies against God and the Church. Have you
ever been referred to as a dog? By church folks? And are you still in
the Church? Well, your faith is great and worthy of emulation. This
woman had such faith. She quickly responded to Jesus: "Truth Lord:
yet the dogs eat of the crumbs which fall from their master's table
(v.27).

This is the response of faith: A refusal to be discouraged by anyone
or anything in pursuit of our desires. In effect, she said, "Lord, I
know healing is "the children's bread," and right now, the children
are those of the House of Israel, but I don't want their bread. I want
only the crumbs that fall. That is good enough for me." She reminds
me of the woman with the "issue of blood" whose faith prompted her

to say, "If I may touch but His clothes, I shall be whole" (Mark 5:28). Just the hem of His clothes! Just the crumbs! God is so big and powerful all we need is the overflow of His grace and glory. Recall how the Israelites could not look at Moses' face after he was in the presence of God for forty days on the mountain? And just think that the radiance was only reflected glory. Jesus finally succumbed to her faith and persistence. "O woman, great is thy faith: be it unto thee even as thou wilt" (v.28). The result: "And her daughter was made whole from that very hour" (v.28).

Before we leave this point, I must note that some people ask, "Isn't it presumptuous to ask God for something when He has already said, No? Yes, it is. But note carefully here, that Jesus never said "No" to this woman. Basically He said, and deliberately so, what the "religionists" were saying, and not what God said. First, Jesus "answered her not a word." Then He told her to whom He was sent. Then He said, "Healing is the children's bread." He never said NO to this woman. At any point, she could have construed Him to mean NO. But she didn't. As far as she was concerned, silence is no answer, and only "No" is "No." The reason many of us do not receive from God is that we construe Him to be saying No when He is not. We put words in His mouth and define what we think He means. Take Eve for example. God said to the first couple, "Of every tree of the garden you may freely eat: but of the tree of the knowledge of good and evil, thou shall not eat of it: for in the day that thou eat thereof thou shall surely die" (Gen.2:16-17). Then Satan came to Eve and subtly asked, "Yea, hath God said, Ye shall not eat of every tree of the garden?" (Gen.3:1). Now listen to Eve's reply: "We may of the fruit of the trees of the garden: but of the fruit of the tree which is in the midst of the garden, God hath said, "ye shall not eat of it, <u>neither shall ye touch it</u>, lest ye die" (Gen.3: 1-3). Note the addition to God's word? Eve assumed that since eating was prohibited, so was touching. But God never placed any prohibition on touching. Refraining from touching the fruit might be the prudent thing to do since that action could lead to temptation, but it was not what God said.

If Eve was in doubt as to what God said, perhaps we could blame it on her memory. But we are not in doubt as to what God is saying to us because we have the written Word of God - the Bible - to which we can always refer. If that Word declares it is God's will to heal everyone - and if the Bible says so - then so be it. We must not try to find hidden meanings in things that are crystal clear, nor should we interpret God's word to justify our frustrations.

From childhood, I struggled with various allergies, and I still do. But I will never give up on God because I know that it is His will to heal me and until He personally appears to me and unequivocally tells me "No", I will continue to hold on to His promise for healing. Call me foolish. My only defense is that I believe in God's word. I do not change doctrines to suit my problems. Like the Canaanite woman, I persevere based on truth.

   vi.   She persisted as if her life depended upon it.

She made her daughter's need her need. Even though it was her daughter who was grievously tormented by a demon, she implored Jesus saying, "have mercy on <u>me</u> O Lord thou Son of David" (v.22). She is a shining example to mothers. She was not going to give her daughter up to the Devil, not without a fight. I know of many fatalists who believe there is nothing they can do about their children's future. Some of them say, "Why bother? When they get to twelve, society takes them. We have no more control over them." Others resign totally. "They will turn out to be what they want to be. Why bother?" But if this woman was going down, it was with her "boots on and pistols smoking." She was prepared to wrestle with the devil, the "church", and even Christ Himself, for the release of her daughter.

She could have been a single mother since there is no mention of a husband or father. Like many single mothers today she could have lamented, "It's tough to raise a child properly, especially when you are all alone." And tough it is. But this woman proves to us that when our faith is firmly entrenched in a loving, merciful, and able God, a partnership is established that will make anything and everything possible.

Conclusion

True faith always prevails. And, when such faith is bolstered with perseverance, it will move mountains, open seas, destroy city walls, subdue kingdoms, obtain promises, stop the mouths of lions, quench the violence of fire, escape the edge of the sword, make the weak strong, put to flight the armies of the enemy, bring the dead to life, endure mocking and scourging, bonds, and imprisonment, and even martyrdom.

In this woman's case, faith and perseverance resulted in her daughter's deliverance from demon possession.

How about you? Are you burdened with a personal problem or even with the problems of a loved one? Are you discouraged? Do you feel like giving up? Well, don't give up because we serve a merciful and powerful God who is able, willing, and ready to meet your need. Your social and economic status and your racial origin are not impediments in your path of blessing. Unbelief is the only obstacle to the blessings of God. Let faith in God come alive in your heart and learn to be patient. Remember, delay does not mean denial. If you can exercise faith and determination like this woman, God will come through for you as he did for her.

> I would not be denied
> I would not be denied
> Till Jesus come and make me whole
> I would not be denied

Rahab
Prostitute to Princess
Story Text: Joshua 2:1-21

And Joshua the son of Nun sent from Shittim two men to spy secretly, saying, Go view the land, even Jericho. And they went, and came into a harlot's house, named Rahab, and lodged there.   And it was told the king of Jericho, saying, Behold, there came men in here tonight of the children of Israel to search out the country. And the king of Jericho sent to Rahab, saying: 'Bring forth the men that have come to thee, who have entered into thy house: for they have come to search out all the country.' And the woman took the two men, and hid them, and said thus, There came men to me, but I knew not where they were: And it came to pass about the time of shutting the gate, when it was dark, that the men went out: where the men went, I know not: pursue after them quickly; for ye shall overtake them.
But she had brought them up to the roof of the house and hid them with the stalks of flax, which she had laid in order upon the roof.
And the men pursued them the way to Jordan to the fords: and as soon as they who pursued them had gone out, they shut the gate.
And before they had lain down, she came up to them upon the roof.
And she said to the men, I know that the LORD hath given you the land, and that your terror hath fallen upon us, and that all the inhabitants of the land faint because of you. For we have heard how the LORD dried up the water of the Red sea for you, when ye came out of Egypt; and what you did to the two kings of the Amorites, that were on the other side of Jordan, Sihon and Og, whom you utterly destroyed. And as soon as we had heard these things, our hearts did melt, neither did there remain any more courage in any man, because of you: for the LORD your God, he is God in heaven above, and in the earth beneath. Now, therefore, I pray you, swear to me by the LORD, since I have showed you kindness, that you will also show kindness to my father's house, and give me a true token:
And that ye will save alive my father, and my mother, and my brethren, and my sisters, and all that they have, and deliver our lives from death.
And the men answered her: Our life for yours if you utter not this our business. And it shall be when the LORD hath given us the land that we will deal kindly and truly with you.

Then she let them down by a cord through the window: for her house was upon the town wall, and she dwelt upon the wall. And she said to them, Depart to the mountain, lest the pursuers meet you; and hide yourselves there three days, until the pursuers have returned: and afterward, you may go your way. And the men said to her: We will be blameless of this thy oath which you have made us swear.

Behold, when we come into the land, you shall bind this line of scarlet thread in the window by which you did let us down: and you shall bring thy father, and your mother, and your brethren, and all your father's household, home to you. And it shall be, that whoever shall go out of the doors of thy house into the street, his blood shall be upon his head, and we will be guiltless: and whoever shall be with you in the house, his blood shall be on our head, if any hand be upon him. And if you shall utter this our business, then we will be free of thy oath that you have made us to swear.

And she said, According to your words, so be it. And she sent them away, and they departed: and she bound the scarlet line in the window.

Many people, Christians included, cannot readily identify with the name "Rahab." And for those who can, she is often nonchalantly dismissed as the prostitute who hid the two spies whom Joshua had commissioned to obtain pre-invasion intelligence on the Canaanite city of Jericho.

Indeed, Rahab's resume is not very impressive to the human eye. She was a Canaanite prostitute who lived in a house on the walls that fortified Jericho. Some scholars believe that two walls, fifteen feet apart, secured the city and that the foundation of Rahab's house straddled the two walls. She dwelt among a people who sacrificed their children to gods of stone and wood, and she herself may have been a temple prostitute, a practitioner of the vile Canaanite religion that fused immorality as a part of worship.

Yet, despite the fact she was a heathen, idol-worshipping prostitute, she demonstrated a faith impressive enough to secure her a place among Israel's heroines of faith. In the book of Hebrews, chapter eleven, her name graces the colonnade of the Hall of Faith, in the company of great saints like Abraham and Moses, while the names of mighty men, like the prophets Daniel and Elijah, are conspicuously absent. In addition, in Matthew, chapter one, - the genealogy of Christ - she is honored to be among the four women named in the Messianic line (v.5). And in the book of James, the apostle cross-references her faith to that of Abraham, "the father of faith," to confirm the doctrine that "faith without works is dead."

It is the purpose of this discourse to probe, with the help of the Holy Spirit, into the mind of God, to understand how and why a promiscuous, heathen harlot was saved and inducted into the honor roll of faith and accorded high honor and acclamation by three major apostles. What was it about this woman that moved God to graft this "wild olive branch" into the impressive lineup that brought Christ to the world? What can we learn from her about God, life, and saving faith?

From the brief and scattered Biblical narratives on "Rahab the harlot," we can learn the following lessons:

1. Rahab admonishes us not to be ashamed of our past.

In all the Biblical narratives concerning Rahab, both before and after
her conversion and assimilation with the people of God, she is
identified as "the harlot." Bearing in mind that all scripture is given
by inspiration of God, it is therefore from the pen of the Holy Spirit,
and not of man, that this appendage comes. In other words, although
God had graciously forgiven Rahab and grafted her into an integral
vein of His redemptive plan, He continued to maintain the reference
to her past profession as a reminder of the difference He made in her
life. Especially, He wants us to be reminded that He is a God of
unlimited grace, eternally enduring mercy, of immeasurable
goodness, and to know that any one of us, despite how corrupted our
lives may have become, is still eligible for salvation and placement
in the program of God to bring Christ to our world.

I know of many Christians who are visibly upset when introduced
with a reference to their past, especially when it was sordid. As far
as they are concerned, the past is gone and forgotten, and there is no
justification for bringing back reminders of bridges burnt, and sinful
practices left behind. Rahab would say, 'complain to God! For if He
was called on to introduce us to an audience, with the intention of
winning others to Himself, assuredly He will make mention of who
and what we were before His saving grace factored into our lives.
How else can He demonstrate the power of His saving grace?' When
we deny our sinful past, we project a lie, that as though by our own
might, skill, willpower, and sense of morality, we are what we have
become. When we remove from our names the appendages of the
past, we deny the grace of God and rob Him of attributable glory and
praise. We diminish His power to save; we deny His power to make
a difference; we frustrate His grace and make "the cross of Christ of
no effect." Our message becomes one that says salvation is through
human potential and not through faith in God. And such heresy God
will not tolerate. He has made it clear, under both dispensations of
Law and Grace that He will not share His glory with any other.
Through the prophet Isaiah, He reminded Israel: "I am the LORD:
that is my name: and my glory will I not give to another, neither my
praise to graven images" (Isaiah 42:8). And through the apostle Paul,
he reminded the Church: "For ye see your calling, brethren, that not

many wise men after the flesh, not many mighty, not many noble, are called: But God hath chosen the foolish things of the world to confound the wise, and God hath chosen the weak things of the world to confound the things which are mighty; And base things of the world, and things which are despised, hath God chosen, and things which are not, to bring to nothing things that are: That no flesh should glory in his presence" (1 Corinthians 1:26-29).

Let us give God the glory and praise that belong to Him and when we so do, we will discover that an uplifted Christ draws more men to the Church than men who exalt themselves.

Jacob was not ashamed to confess he was a "worm" and "deceiver" even after he was crowned a "prince with God" and given "power with men." He knew that if anyone attempted to bridge the gap between the "deceiver" and the "prince," they will discover the grace of God as the reconciling item, and the praise and glory will naturally shift from him to the One who effected that reconciliation.

Likewise, even after her redemption from a sinful life, her subsequent marriage to Salmon, one of the Israeli spies, and her grafting into the Messianic line, Rahab had no objections to the reference as "the harlot." As the happily married wife and mother cradled her baby and looked into his eyes, knowing that she, once a renowned prostitute, had been chosen to be a progenitor of the Messiah, she must have wept with uncontrollable joy and gratitude. And most assuredly, if she is permitted to speak to us today, especially those who deny their past and burn their bridges, she will exhort us to share our life experience as it was before conversion, as a testimony to the power of God to save, and not to deny it, for it is still the most potent of messages in the arsenal of any believer.

2. Rahab reminds us that salvation is never dependent on human goodness.

Worthy of more than a passing glance is the fact that of the four women listed in the Messianic genealogy, three of them, including Rahab, were adulteresses. Some Biblical scholars and theologians, to explain the honorable references accorded a treacherous prostitute, conclude that the word "harlot" as used in those days, referred also to an "innkeeper," and therefore it should be interpreted that Rahab's profession was of such a nature. This interpretation is dubious for several reasons. First, it is purely speculative - not all theologians agree. Second, those who interpret "Rahab the harlot" to mean "Rahab the innkeeper", must be consistent in their explanation of the other adulteresses, not only in the genealogy of Christ but also in all such biblical references. Are they all innkeepers? And what about other sins like murder and extortion? Is the murderer more worthy of salvation than the harlot? And are we to find some explanation for David's double sin of adultery and murder to justify his appendage as a "man after God's own heart?" One can easily see how foolish it is to attempt to justify the acceptance of every sinner in the Bible with an explanation other than grace, the unearned favor of God. Last but certainly not least, this explanation must be rejected because it shoots at the heart of a gracious God. It attempts to nullify God's saving grace.

The truth is that though there is mental and intellectual assent to the doctrine of salvation by grace, humans struggle to accept the fact that the vile and wretched can come to God on the same terms as the morally upright. They simply cannot accept the fact that all men are saved "by grace and not of works which we have done," and so they derive some stupid explanation to justify their position. They seem to forget that "grace" means unmerited favor, and that salvation is wholly and absolutely an act of grace. Does it mean then that God condones sinful practices? Certainly not! But it does mean that His mercy and forgiveness are available to everyone, regardless of the extent, duration, or potency of their sinfulness. Rahab's salvation and elevation to a place of honor is the classic argument for the grace of God and His "so great salvation."

Great indeed is the temptation to boast of our Christian heritage or of a good moral lifestyle to which we were privileged, as though God was obligated to act on our behalf because of any of these factors. I have heard so many people boast like the rich young ruler did, of their works of righteousness and diligent observance of the "golden rule" from their youth, tacitly intimating that they deserved salvation, and how often I hear Jesus say, "You are not far from the kingdom of heaven."

Still, others compare themselves to men of lesser morality, as the Pharisee did to the Publican, and say, I am not like that Publican over there. I fast and pray and pay tithes and go to church regularly, I deserve salvation and special honor. And how often we are reminded of the words of Jesus that the publican went home justified but the Pharisee remained under condemnation. In fact, Jesus taught that the Publicans and harlots will enter the kingdom of God and will share equally in all its privileges (Matt.21: 31), while many of the children of the kingdom, because they trusted in their heritage for salvation, will find themselves expelled into outer darkness where there will be wailing and gnashing of teeth.

Rahab reminds us that the worse of sin is no match for the strength of Divine grace; that as long as there is genuine repentance there is no sin too big for God to forgive. Some of the greatest saints have confessed to deeds of infamy and a life of vice before their confrontation with the Lord. Saul made havoc on the Church, hauling many men and women to prison, and witnessing the death of others. Yet the Lord saved him and made him who was the "chief of sinners" the "chief of apostles." Jacob, a deceiver, and trickster all his life, was transformed into a "prince with God." Peter, a fisherman who swore, lied, and denied his Master, was transformed into a courageous preacher of truth when he bowed to the Lordship of Jesus.

For all who surrender to the Lordship of Jesus Christ and to the saving grace of God, the end of the story is always the same - forgiveness and exaltation. Rahab lived a life of sin, but she believed that the arms of pardon were not beyond her reaching, turned her back on her way of life, and grabbed on to the hands of redeeming grace. Somehow, she learned one of the most comforting truths of all - that "where sin abounds, grace did much more abound."

3. Rahab reminds us that God is no respecter of persons.

From the days of Abraham to the time of Christ, the Jewish nation wholeheartedly believed that Jehovah God was their exclusive property; that His power was theirs to be used to defeat their enemies, and that His grace, mercy, and goodness, were theirs alone to appropriate for a full and abundant life. Accordingly, they did everything possible to prevent others from sharing the equalizing grace and love of God. For instance, when Jonah was commissioned to preach repentance to the city of Nineveh, he flatly refused the assignment and attempted to flee the presence of the Lord. Deep down in his heart, he suspected that the Gentile city might come to repentance and be saved from destruction, and that possibility he refused to accept because the Ninevites were instrumental in killing thousands of his people. They, of all people, must not share in Israel's covenant relationship with God, and if they must, he will not be a part of the process.

Today, the Church is still prejudiced against the vile and the outsider. In many congregations and denominations, believers are still judged by their color, creed, and culture to determine whether or not they are acceptable for membership or eligible for certain offices. When it comes to the evangelism of the lost, for example, many churches will consciously program their activities to go around their "Samarias" for fear of having any dealings with people unlike themselves. On the individual level, many believers are like Jonah, refusing to take the gospel to certain individuals for fear that they might believe and be saved and come to share in the blessings of Christ. On the other hand, when a sincere believer decides to break the barriers, he may face ridicule and exclusion. The apostle Peter, a Jew, was commissioned to take the gospel to the home of Cornelius, a Gentile, and to alleviate his fears and remove inherent misconceptions concerning those outside the commonwealth of Israel, God gave him a vision of a bundle let down with all kinds of living creatures: four-footed animals, reptiles of the earth, and birds of the air - making up the three classifications of the whole animal kingdom - and commanded him to eat. He protested until God rebuked him, saying, "What God hath cleansed, let no man call unclean." Peter's initial reluctance to go to the Gentiles stemmed from the fact that he knew the message of the vision was not specific to foods alone, for later, at the home of Cornelius, he told the gathering that God has shown to him that he should not call anything or anyone impure or unclean (Acts 10: 28). How we need to hear those words again and again! Lord, let down the blanket once more! We need that vision to execute and expedite the "Great Commission" to preach the gospel to all peoples and all nations.

The conversion of Rahab and her inclusion in the lineage of Christ, assures us that Almighty God never had, and never will have since He is a just and immutable Being, any preference for one individual or race or color over another. As Creator of all men, He treats us all equally. Thus, in every nation, all those who fear Him and do His will are accepted by Him.

4. Rahab confirms that salvation comes through faith in the word of God.

We note the orderly working of Divine providence in leading the spies to the unlikely home of Rahab. Since merchants and others frequented her place, it was a strategic ploy to avoid suspicion by the local authorities. Soon after their arrival, the spies learned why Rahab was so disposed toward them. She said, "I know Jehovah hath given...Jehovah dried up the Red Sea... He is the God of heaven above and the earth beneath..." It was clear that she heard the Word and believed it with all sincerity.

It is no secret that multitudes of common people experience miracles of healing and salvation because of their simple and child-like faith in the Word of God, while others who profess a deeper understanding of the Word, like the Scribes and Pharisees, are unable to appropriate its blessings and must go away empty and disappointed. Rahab proves that great faith is not dependent on a great amount of truth. She heard only a few sermon lines: "How the Lord dried up the water of the Red Sea for you," and "what ye did to the two kings of the Amorites" (Jo.2:10), but that was enough preaching to make her heart "melt" and desire the protection of the God of Israel.

In this, she proves convincingly that one does not require much knowledge of God to generate saving faith, and that no one will be excused on the ground that they received too little "light," or that they did not have enough biblical exposition or clarification or convincing concerning the need for salvation. The truth is that most of those who rail against the claims of Christ and Christianity do so only to deflect from the need for personal commitment. Some pretend to have genuine concerns that must be resolved before a commitment is made, but in effect, they seek a deferment of salvation to pursue their personal agenda. A non-Christian girl once told me at the outset of my attempt to share with her the gospel, "It matters not what you say to me because my mind is already made up." Others fear the truth will lead to excommunication and isolation, so they pay no attention to it. Others, like philosophers, are only interested in religion so far as it contributes to the heap of unanswerable questions. For them, truth is a frustration. It robs them of the sensual high that comes from a life of continuous contemplation.

Arguably, we have far more light than Rahab, far more light than the disciples who abandoned all to follow Jesus, and far more light than many of those who received miracles of healing and deliverance at the hands of Jesus. In fact, it can be said that the Old Testament saints had only half the light of those in the New. They lived in the shadow of the corporeal; in the symbolism of the real; in the type of the actual; and in the likeness of the authentic. Yet, the little fragment of truth they received was enough to generate in them blessed saving faith.

Rahab heard a few words about the great and awesome power of the Lord, believed it, and was saved. Today, we have access to the whole Bible, the full revelation of God, the substance of things hoped for, the fulfillment of all prophecies, and the materializing of all Old Testament shadows. We hear the Word of God on television, radio, in published media, and from church pulpits. How can anyone be excused on the grounds of ignorance? Will not the Queen of Sheba rise in judgment against our generation because we had a "greater than Solomon?" And will not the children of Nineveh rise in condemnation of this generation because we had a "greater than Jonah?"

Jonah preached a sermon of eight words and the vast city of Nineveh, likened to modern Manhattan, New York, repented and was saved. How then can anyone be excused on the grounds that they had but little light? Those who read these words and reject Christ are without excuse, for on the Day of Judgment, these very words will testify against you.

Like Rahab, we must have unquestionable faith in the Word of God. It is not our place to question but to believe. The writer of Hebrews cautions the seeker: "He that comes to God must first believe that He is." In other words, we must accept His existence by faith in His Word that says "He is." If He convicts us as sinners under judgment, then so are we. And if He declares the availability of salvation through faith in Christ, then so it is!

5. Rahab demonstrates the working of true faith.

In every dispensation since the fall of man, faith has always been the way of blessing and the means of salvation. Contrary to what many are taught, the Old Testament saints were not saved by the observance of laws and commandments but by an abiding faith in the promised Messiah. Abraham, an Old Testament saint, was called the father of faith, and all the men and women listed in Hebrews chapter 11, were Old Testament saints who lived and died in faith. The Scriptures teach that the just are saved by faith; sanctified by faith (Acts 26:18); justified by faith (Romans 3:28); stand by faith (Romans 11:20); walk by faith (2Corinthians 5:7); live by faith (Galatians 2:20); overcome the world by faith (1John 5:4), and they die in faith (Hebrews 11). The Bible also teaches that faith assures success (Mk 11:2; Lk.8:50); is a fundamental duty (John 6:28, 29); is a defensive weapon (Eph.6:16); is essential in prayer (Jas.1:5, 6); and should be united with love (1Jo 3:23). Indeed, "without faith it is impossible to please God" (Hebrews 11:1). But the Church needs to be reminded again and again that faith manifests itself in action, function, toil, and performance. We need to be constantly reminded that although our works of righteousness are not the basis of salvation, they become the basis for our eternal rewards and commendations. We will be rewarded at the Judgment Seat of Christ based on our works, and if there are no works worthy of reward, we will suffer loss.

The apostle James notes that "faith without works is dead," and quotes the works of Rahab as an example of the operation of faith.

> Likewise, also was not Rahab the harlot justified by works when she had received the messengers and had sent them out another way? (James 2:25).

James tells us that it was by faith she received the spies and gave them refuge even though their king and country had declared war on the Israelites, and even though she herself, from her own confession, knew their purpose was to invade her country. She hid them with flax on the roof of her house and when interrogated by city officials denied having done so. She lied, betraying king and country, yet, according to the apostle James (2:25), she is "justified by works," and specifically so in that "she received the messengers and sent them out another way." How can this anomaly be explained? In what way were her works justified? The case is extraordinary, to say the least, and should not be hurriedly taken to be a precedent. And as someone pointed out, the Scriptures justify her deeds and not her words. Therefore the answer must be that because she knew the Lord had given Israel the land (v.9), her obligations to God took precedence over her obligations to man and country, and it would have been a sin for her to join with others who hindered them from possessing what God, the Creator, and Owner of all things, had bestowed to them.

Rahab exposed herself to deadly peril in obedience to faith. She heard how the God of Israel had drowned the armies of Pharaoh in the Red Sea and how He brought them out with a mighty hand, defeating all their enemies along the way. And she believed that He who had begun a work is able to complete it; that regardless of the efforts of the people of Jericho, the Hebrews will occupy the land. It was on the ground of God's faithfulness, grace, and power that she placed her faith, and it was that faith that justified the works done on the behalf of the children of Israel.

6. Rahab reminds us that often we must dare to stand alone.

The philosophy of our world is that there is safety in numbers; that it is unpopular and even dangerous to stand alone on any issue. Jesus however, refuted this teaching in both doctrine and practice. He taught that the majority is not always right, and in fact, that the road that leads to destruction is "broad, and many be there that go in thereat," whereas the road that leads to life is "narrow, and few be there that find it." Hence, and especially with regards to salvation, it is immeasurably dangerous to trust in a doctrine or philosophy simply because the majority believes in it. Truth allows no compromise whatsoever. It does not care for popularity, acceptance, support, or confirmation. It is not strengthened or comforted by a majority affirmation. Truth is a majority. And, contrary to some contemporary teachings, truth is not relative. It is a holy and immutable Person - Jesus Christ (Jn.14: 6). Thus, if we live according to the Word of God, we live in truth; as long as we walk according to its principles, we walk in truth; and as long as our confession is in harmony with the Word of God, we speak the truth.

History, both Biblical and secular, has taught us that those who made a difference in their world are those who dared to stand firm on their convictions even if it meant standing alone. David, a shepherd boy, stood alone against the feared Philistine warrior, Goliath, and saved the nation of Israel. Elijah stood alone against the prophets of Baal on Mount Carmel and won a decisive victory for the Lord of hosts. We must dare to believe the Word of God and dare to stand firmly on its principles and precepts, even if it means being alone. For in a true sense we are not. We are on God's side, and He will vindicate and honor our stand for the Truth.

Rahab was aware of the dangers that awaited her if she was caught hoarding the spies in her home and releasing to them information vital to the security of the city, but she had nothing to lose. If the city officials did not put her to death, she would have been buried under the ruins of Jericho anyway. She took her chance on God and it paid her well.

Jesus reminds us that, "if we save our life we will lose it, but if we lose it for His sake, we will find it." Rahab preferred to lose her life for the God of Israel and save it eternally, rather than to save it for the king and people of Jericho temporarily and lose it eternally. In the end, she stood alone amid the crumbling bricks and ascending clouds of dust.

7. Rahab's deliverance confirms that the righteous will be spared from the coming judgment.

Prior to the invasion of Jericho, Joshua instructed his men: "And the city shall be accursed, even it, and all that is in it, to the Lord: only Rahab the harlot shall live, she and all that are with her in the house, because she hid the messengers that we sent" (Joshua 6:17).

Through the centuries many have promulgated the doctrine that believers must and will go through the terrible seven-year period called the Great Tribulation. They explain that it is necessary for the Church to be purified and only the sufferings of the seven-year Tribulation can purge the bride of Christ and make her ready for marriage to the Lamb. They seem to have forgotten about the efficacy of the blood of Jesus Christ to redeem, sanctify, and justify the sinner.

Others argue for a partial rapture theory. Their hypothesis is that the spiritual believers will be removed, and the carnal will be left for purification. The question they need to answer is: How can the marriage of the Lamb and his bride take place when part of the bride is left behind? Harold Wilmington observed:

> The Bible teaches clearly that the rapture is pre-tribulational in nature and includes all believers. See 1 Thessalonians 1:10 and Romans 5:9. Perhaps the strongest proof of this statement is the fact that up to chapter 6 of Revelation the church is mentioned many times, but from chapter 6 to chapter 19 (the period of the Tribulation), there is no mention whatsoever of the church on earth." He notes also, "We are told that Christians are God's ambassadors on earth (2

Corinthians 5:20), and that he will someday declare war on this earth. The first thing a king or president does after he declares war on another country is to call his ambassadors home (*The King is Coming*).

In addition, Dr. John Valvoord listed fifty arguments to prove that the righteous will be removed before the Tribulation. Some of these include:

- None of the Old Testament passages on the Tribulation mention the Church (Dan.4:29, 30; Jer.30:4-11; Dan.8: 24-27; 12:1, 2).
- None of the New Testament passages on the Tribulation mention the Church (Mt.13:30; 39-42, 48-50; 24:15-31; 1Thess.1:9, 10; 5:4-9; 2 Thess.2:1-11; Rev.4-18).
- The Church is not appointed to wrath (Ro.4:9; 1Thess.1:9, 10; 5:9).
- It is characteristic of divine dealing to deliver believers before a divine judgment is inflicted on the world (2Pe.2:5-9).
- The Holy Spirit as the restrainer must be taken out of the world before the "lawless one," who dominates the Tribulation period, can be revealed (2Thess.2:6-8).
- The coming of Christ for His bride must take place before the Second Coming to the earth for the wedding feast (Rev.19:7-10).
- According to 2 Corinthians 5:10, all believers in this age must appear before the Judgment Seat of Christ.

As can be easily seen, those who insist that the righteous must suffer the Great Tribulation simply miss the message of the scriptures - one that consistently teaches that the righteous will be separated from the sinful before judgment is executed. Lot was delivered from Sodom before fire and brimstone annihilated the city; Enoch was removed before the Flood; Noah was lifted up in the ark before the great Flood inundated the world and took the life of every living thing, and John the Revelator was called to "come up" before the apocalyptic judgments were poured out on an unbelieving world.

So too, those who "vex their righteous soul with the unlawful deeds" of this world, and enter into Jesus, the Ark of safety, will not be touched by fire or by flood but shall be caught up and away from this world before the wrath of God is unleashed. The Lord promised "Rahab shall live," and He fulfilled His word. Similarly, He has promised that we who are in Christ "shall be saved from wrath." And He will fulfill His promise.

8. Rahab reminds us of our responsibility for evangelism.

Since the fall of man, God has consistently indicated that we are our brother's keepers, and that failure to honor that responsibility to our fellow man will draw certain judgment. Consider the following passages:

> And surely your blood will I require; at the hand of every beast will I require it, and at the hand of man; at the hand of every man's brother will I require the life of man (Genesis 9:5).

> When I say to the wicked, Thou shall surely die; and thou give him not warning, nor speak to warn the wicked from his wicked way, to save his life; the same wicked man shall die in his iniquity, but his blood will I require at thy hand (Ezekiel 3:18 and repeated almost verbatim in Ezekiel 33:8).

> But if the watchman shall see the sword come, and blow not the trumpet, and the people be not warned; if the sword shall come, and take any person from among them, he is taken away in his iniquity; but his blood will I require at the watchman's hand (Ezekiel 33:6).

Our responsibility to the lost is clear: we must warn them of coming judgment, and we must do so regardless of how we feel towards them. The little maid who served in the household of Naaman the Syrian was a spoil of war. Naaman had likely killed her parents yet when she heard of her master's affliction with deadly leprosy and had every justifiable reason to gloat, she did no such thing. Instead, she used the opportunity to inform Naaman of the availability of saving grace in Israel. Likewise, Paul and Silas, unjustly accused, cruelly abused, and roughly thrown in prison, instead of entertaining vengeful thoughts, sought the opportunity to use their captivity as a key to the freedom of others.

Rahab begs us to hasten to the rescue of those we love to ensure they are removed from the place of destruction and given an opportunity to share in the blessedness of salvation. She was a harlot, despised by society, and likely despised by her own family. Yet, when it came to the salvation of the soul, she understood her responsibility to share the light and the blessing she received with her household. And that responsibility was well discharged. As the smoke cleared, she and her household were the only ones left standing.

9. Rahab confirms that God rewards every work done in his name and for His glory.

Rahab helped the people of God and in so doing was abundantly blessed by Him. She was not only brought into fellowship with the household of Israel, but she was privileged to be a part of the ancestry of Jesus. Some teachers believed she might have married Salmon, one of the spies she hoarded. Her son, Boaz (Matthew 1:5), married Ruth the Moabitess, and they became the grandparents of David, the progenitor of Christ (Matthew 1:16).

Her petition to Israel was just and reasonable. She had protected them, now they must protect her. As a result of protecting the two spies, she spared the entire nation of Israel an unwanted setback. Her kindness transcended those directly helped. So too, their kindness to her must extend beyond her to include her family as well. Rahab never dreamt that she would find herself in the lineage of Christ. That she, a Canaanite harlot would be happily married to an Israelite prince and be grafted into the plan of God in such an enviable manner was beyond her greatest expectations. But she was, enforcing the truth that they that show mercy will receive mercy and that the repercussions of one's acts of kindness must never be underestimated.

Likewise, when we faithfully serve the Lord and step out in faith to honor Him and advance His cause, He will not only protect us from our enemies but will graft us into the body of Christ, where, in "the ages to come He might show the exceeding riches of His grace in His kindness toward us." The rewards for faithful spiritual service are as follows:

- For soul-winners: "And they that are wise shall shine as the brightness of the firmament, and they that turn many to righteousness as the stars forever and ever" (Daniel 12:3).
- For humble servants: "And whoever shall give to drink to one of these little ones a cup of cold water only in the name of a disciple, verily I say to you, he shall by no means lose his reward" (Matthew 10:42).
- For faithful stewards: "His lord said to him, Well done, good and faithful servant; thou hast been faithful over a few things, I will make thee ruler over many things: enter thou into the joy of thy lord" (Matthew 25:23).
- For the benevolent: "But love ye your enemies, and do good and lend, hoping for nothing again; and your reward shall be great, and ye shall be the children of the Highest: for he is kind to the unthankful and to the evil" (Luke 6:35).
- For the good of all nations: "But glory, honor, and peace, to every man that works good, to the Jew first, and also to the Greek" (Romans 2:10).
- For all ranks and stations: "Now he that plants and he that waters are one: and every man shall receive his own reward according to his own labor" (1Corinthians 3:8). "Knowing that whatever good thing any man doeth, the same shall he receive from the Lord, whether he be bond or free" (Ephesians 6:8).

So, "let us not be weary in well-doing: for in due season we shall reap if we faint not. As we have therefore opportunity, let us do good unto all men, especially unto them who are of the household of faith" (Gal.6:9, 10).

10. Rahab cautions us to remember that salvation is conditional.

Rahab reminds us that the promise of protection and salvation is conditional upon us maintaining a life of continuous fellowship with God based on the covenant that was sealed with the blood of His Son. She must tie the scarlet cord with which she let down the spies out of the window and let it remain visible so that when the advancing Israeli armies arrive on the scene, they will see the easily visible sign and spare her house from violence and destruction. A similar procedure was followed prior to the exodus of the Hebrews from Egypt. The Hebrews were commanded to mark their doorposts and lintels with the blood of a lamb so that when the angels of death pass over he will be able to distinguish those homes that are to be spared destruction.

Through the centuries, the issue of the security of salvation has been a thorn in some of the best theological minds. It is not practical to discuss all the arguments for and against "eternal security," in this section, but only to include a few salient points.

The doctrine of eternal salvation owes its origins to St. Augustine and John Calvin who claimed that it was simply their interpretation of Paul's teaching. Essentially, they maintain that salvation is entirely of God and has nothing to do with man. Calvin explains: "Predestination is the eternal decree of God, by which He has decided what is to become of each individual. For all are not created in like condition; but eternal life is foreordained for some, eternal condemnation for others." Hence the deductions are drawn that man has no say in whether he can or would be saved, and if God chooses to save someone, then that person, having no say in the matter, can never be lost. Those who oppose that doctrine, me included, take the Armenian view which states that God's will is to save all men because Christ died for all (1Ti.2: 4-6; He.2: 9; 2Co.5:14; Tit.2:11, 12), and to that end, He offers His grace to all. In other words, while salvation is the free gift of God to man, the latter has certain conditions and requirements to fulfill if he will benefit from that offer. He can choose either to accept or to reject it. The power of choice remains his alone. The scriptures do teach predestination in the sense that God, because of His foreknowledge, foresees those persons who will accept His offer of salvation and thus be saved, and predestines them to that heavenly inheritance. In the words of Myer Pearlman, "He foreknew their destiny but did not fix it."

Experience has taught us that it is possible to fall from grace, a condition called "backsliding." Because of free will, it is possible to resist the grace of God to the point of eternal loss (Jn.6:40; Heb.6:4-6; 2 Pe.2:21), and it is possible to refuse His offer of salvation even after initial acceptance (Heb.10:26-29). The sum of the matter then is that God offers salvation freely to all men and wishes that all men will receive that offer and be saved, but man, with a free will, has the responsibility to accept or reject that offer, and in that sense is the governor of his own destiny.

As Rahab was responsible to obey the conditions of her salvation, that is, to always keep the scarlet cord visible, the Christian is responsible for "working out his salvation with fear and trembling" (Phil.2:12). He must abide in Christ, live in obedience to the Word of God, and maintain his protection from spiritual death by ensuring he is "marked," having his heart cleansed, and his conscience sprinkled with the blood of Jesus.

11. Rahab reminds us that there will always be a remnant of godly people.

In the opinion of the government and the citizens of Jericho, there was absolutely nothing to worry about. Their city was well secured with both man-made and natural fortifications. The treacherous waters of the Jordan River protected them on one side and impenetrable walls all around the city safeguarded the other side. As such, they lived in absolute indifference to any threat of impending judgment. The sun rose, as usual, every morning; commerce and industry thrived; the children played as usual; they built and planted; they married and were given in marriage; the newspapers carried news of peace and tranquility everywhere; life went on as usual, there was no cause for alarm. Yet, despite the apparent peace that was enjoyed by the residents of Jericho, there was one person who believed that impending judgment hung over the city. She knew that the iniquity of her people was full; that they were indifferent to God and their need for His salvation, and that it was only a matter of time before the inevitable occurred. Rahab heard of the judgments of God on the Egyptians and all who opposed His people and His purposes, but so did the rest of the people of Jericho. The difference between them is that she did not ignore the threat of impending judgment because there was world peace, because Jericho prospered, or because the city was fortified with walls so wide, she could build her house on it. She believed the Word of God - that unless they repented and turned to the one true God, they will suffer incalculable loss. That was the nature of the faith that won her a place among the great saints.

She serves as a pointed reminder to our generation that the coming of Christ to execute judgment on the world of the ungodly is not dependent on the occurrence of wars and rumors of wars, or earthquakes and pestilence and famine. Christ will come because He said He would. The world will be judged because Christ said it would be judged. The sad truth is that Jericho was indifferent to God and judgment on sin because they were deluded by the peace and prosperity of the times. Remarkably, Jesus predicted the existence of similar political and economic conditions when He returns to judge the world.

> For yourselves know perfectly that the day of the Lord so cometh as a thief in the night. For when they shall say, Peace and safety; then sudden destruction cometh upon them, as travail upon a woman with child; and they shall not escape (1Thess.5:2, 3).

A common delusion among many Christians today is the belief that something calamitous must occur to usher in the return of Christ. So they look for calamities around the world and decide whether it is serious enough for them to get busy in the work of the kingdom. But Rahab will warn us that judgment can come in the most unlikely of times. For her to have proclaimed to her city a message of impending judgment would have drawn mockery and derision. Who would have believed a harlot's report? Equally, those who look for symptoms that indicate "right conditions" for the return of Jesus will be caught "naked and ashamed" when He makes His appearance. Hence, the apostle cautions:

> But ye, brethren, are not in darkness, that day should overtake you as a thief. Ye are all children of light, and children of the day: we are not of the night, nor of darkness. Therefore let us not sleep, as do others; but let us watch and be sober-minded...putting on the breastplate of faith and love; and for a helmet, the hope of salvation (1Thess.5:4-6, 8).

In this she cautions us to be always prepared - good or bad; to be awake and to watch - day and night; to live by faith in the Word of God - despite contrary reasoning; and to patiently await the sure hope of salvation, even if all others perish.

12. Rahab confirms that God will bring to himself all genuine searchers for truth.

Several years ago I was asked to sit in on a panel at a dental auxiliary school to answer questions on Biblical teachings. One hygienist stood up and asked me the first question. She asked: Do you believe that only Christians will be saved? And if so, what about all the other sincere and religious people around the world? I was a young believer then, just a few months old in Christ, and I did not have a ready answer to her question. With everyone looking at me, my mind just went blank, and all I could do was utter a silent prayer of desperation. I prayed, Lord, there must be an answer. Please help me find it!

Then, in a flash of inspiration, I said, I believe that if anyone is truly and sincerely desirous of knowing God, the Lord will reveal Himself to that person. Immediately, the conversion story of Cornelius and his household came to my mind. I told them how Cornelius, a centurion, came to the knowledge of salvation in Christ. That even though he was a "devout man, and one that feared God with all his house, who gave many alms to the people, and prayed to God always," his sincerity did not bring him acceptance with God. But what it did do was to move God to bring him to the knowledge of the truth. Consequently, an angel came to him and said, "Cornelius, your prayers and your alms are come up for a memorial before God. And now, send men to Joppa, and call for one Simon...he shall tell you what you ought to do." Eventually, Peter came to Cornelius's home and preached the gospel of Jesus Christ, and Cornelius and his household were saved and filled with the Holy Ghost (Acts 10).

That day I left the panel discussion knowing in my heart that it was the Lord who had revealed His word to me. Today, twenty years later (1996), my answer to all seekers is the same. If you are sincerely desirous of knowing Christ and His salvation, God will make a way for you. Rahab lived amid sin and ignorance, but in her heart, she longed for deliverance. And the Lord revealed Himself to her. The Bible reveals God as a God of the individual. One who may be pushed and jostled by a multitude of people but who still senses the touch of faith on the hem of His garment; One who may be surrounded by the deafening cries of a crowd but who still hears the cry of faith from a poor, blind beggar sitting by the wayside. All who hunger and thirst for righteousness will be filled, and all who seek Him will find Him. The question that you need to ask is, Am I desirous of finding God? And if you are, why not give Jesus a chance to prove to you that He is the Way, the Truth, and the Life? You have nothing to lose but everything to gain.

13. Rahab reminds us of the effectiveness of intercessory prayer.

She asked not only for her safety but for that of her family as well. And God honored her request to the extent of "our life for yours." She proves there is power in intercession. If someone you love is lost in sin, dwells in an ill-fated environment, or is being tempted and "sifted," don't give up on them. Intercede for them! Fight for them, on your knees! They may be helpless in themselves but not when you are allied with them in battle. Remember, the "effectual, fervent prayer of a righteous man avails much."

The Bible records many instances of the efficacy of intercessory prayer. These include Moses for Israel (Ex.32:32); Moses for

Miriam (Nu.12:13); Samuel for Israel (1Sa.7:5); a man of God for Jeroboam (1Ki.13:6); David for Israel (1Ch.21:17); Hezekiah for the People (2Ch.30:18); Job for his friends (Job 42:10); and Paul for the Christians at Ephesus (Eph1:16). Finally, Christ, the exegesis of all truth, taught us the power and efficacy of intercessor prayer. He interceded:

- For Sinners: "Therefore I will divide to him a portion with the great, and he shall divide the spoil with the strong; because he hath poured out his soul to death: and he was numbered with the transgressors, and he bore the sin of many and made intercession for the transgressors" (Isaiah 53:12).
- For Weak Believers: "But I have prayed for thee, that thy faith fails not: and when thou art converted, strengthen thy brethren" (Luke 22:32).
- For Enemies: "Then said Jesus, Father, forgive them; for they know not what they do. And they parted his raiment and cast lots" (Luke 23:34).
- For Sending of the Comforter: "And I will pray to the Father, and he shall give you another Comforter, that he may abide with you forever" (John 14:16).
- For the Church: "I pray for them: I pray not for the world, but for them whom thou hast given to me; for they are yours" (John 17:9).
- For Our Acceptance with God: "Who is he that condemns? It is Christ that died, or rather, that is risen again, who is even at the right hand of God, who also makes intercession for us" (Romans 8:34).
- For our Salvation: "Wherefore he is able also to save them to the uttermost that come to God by him, seeing he ever lives to make intercession for them" (Hebrews 7:25).

Intercession works! Let us continue to intercede for our friends and our enemies so that they too might be saved.

14. Rahab reminds us that judgment will be executed against sin.

Earlier, Joshua had sent out the spies to help him plan the strategies for his military campaign against Jericho. But the chief purpose of their report was to show the spiritual condition of the people. Their reconnaissance revealed that the iniquity of Jericho was full. The city enjoyed outward peace and tranquility, its economy was prosperous, it was environmentally conscious, it fostered social harmony and universal brotherhood, and it respected all lifestyles. But there was spiritual degeneracy in the land. And if there was spiritual decay, the city was ripe for judgment. Rahab did not question the reason for the overthrow of the other nations, nor did she question the reason for the overthrow of her own city. She knew like all sinners and sinning societies know, that unless they repented and returned to the one true God, nations and individuals that forget God will soon be forgotten of God.

Of course, there may be no outward indication of defeat in your life. You may be prosperous, and successful, with a great family and bright-looking future, but the truth is that as long as you are without Christ, you are dead in trespasses and sins, you are blinded by the god of this world, and you are led by the spirit of disobedience, and the judgment of God hangs ominously over your life.

15. Rahab reminds us that the world is not ignorant of what goes on in the church.

How surprised the spies might have been to learn that common, heathen people in a land across the river knew in sufficient detail the acts of the Church from the time they left Egypt. It was no secret to them that the "Lord dried up the water of the Red Sea" for His people, and that the Lord had vanquished "the two kings of the Amorites that were on the other side of Jordan."

Rahab's confession to the spies in this regard cautions saints to a life of purity and Christ-likeness. It reminds us that we are under observation and scrutiny by opposing forces, visible and invisible. The apostle Paul had this awareness when he wrote: "Ye are our epistles, read and known of all men." Observe, he said, "all men." In other words, our religion is no secret and the way we live is no secret. The things God does for us are disseminated among the heathen religions, and the actions of the church are noted with careful diligence by innumerable hosts. And it is with this consciousness we must live if we hope to win our world for Christ. We must set a watch on our lips lest the enemy hears confessions of unbelief rather than of faith. We must "let our lights so shine before men that they may see our good works and glorify our Father which is in heaven." We must walk worthy of our calling. Our lives must be intrinsically connected to the Divine life so that the glory that comes from our victories and successes will be directed to the One to whom belongs all the glory and praise.

16. Rahab reminds us that salvation is through the divinely prescribed sacrifice.

As Israel needed the scarlet blood of the lamb on their doorposts to protect them from the angel of death, so Rahab needed the scarlet cord so that she might be distinguished from the others and be spared from the destruction to befall Jericho. She reminds us of the need for the scarlet blood of Christ, the ultimate Lamb of God, to be applied on the doorposts and lintels of our hearts so that we might be spared from wrath to come.

Even today, many worshippers around the world continue to offer blood - the blood of animals, as a sacrifice for sin. But the blood of animals is not efficacious for sin for the following reasons:

- There is little relationship between the offeror and the offeree, between man-made in the image and the likeness of God and an irrational and irresponsible creature.
- The animal does not offer itself voluntarily or intelligently but must be dragged to the slaughter without a clue as to why it is thus being led.
- The death of an animal could not exercise any spiritual power on the inner man. Its blood could not remove the guilt of sin or bring peace to an accusing conscience.
- The blood of the animal itself is corrupted by sin, and therefore is a poor substitute as a sacrifice.
- Animal sacrifices "sanctifies to the purifying of the flesh"

(He.9:13). That is, they atoned for the outward acts of sin and contained no spiritual virtue.

- The fact that animal sacrifices must be repeated proves their ineffectiveness to "make the worshipper perfect" (He.10:1, 2).

Hence the writer of Hebrews sums up: "For it is not possible that the blood of bulls and of goats should take away sins...but this man (Jesus), after he had offered one sacrifice for sins forever, sat down on the right hand of God" (Heb.10:4,11,12). This one sacrifice of Jesus Christ provides:

- Remission of sins: "For this is my blood of the new testament, which is shed for many for the remission of sins" (Matthew 26:28).
- Redemption: "Forasmuch as ye know that ye were not redeemed with corruptible things, as silver and gold, from your vain way of life received by tradition from your fathers; But with the precious blood of Christ, as of a lamb without blemish and without spot" (1Peter 1:18, 19).
- Acceptance in the Divine family: "He that eats my flesh, and drinks my blood, dwells in me, and I in him" (John 6:56).
- Justification: "Much more then, being now justified by his blood, we shall be saved from wrath through him" (Romans 5:9).
- Peace: "And, having made peace through the blood of his cross, by him to reconcile all things to himself; by him, I say, whether they are things on earth, or things in heaven" (Colossians 1:20).
- Sanctification: "How much more shall the blood of Christ, who through the eternal Spirit offered himself without spot to God, cleanse your conscience from dead works to serve the living God?" (Heb.9:14).
- Victory over the powers of darkness: "And they overcame him by the blood of the Lamb, and by the word of their testimony; and they loved not their lives to the death" (Rev.12:11).

As Rahab needed the scarlet chord to ensure her salvation, so we need the blood of Jesus to atone for our sins, to bond us with the Divine family, to make peace with God, to continually cleanse us from sin, and to ensure continuous victory over sin and evil.

Therefore, without the scarlet blood of Christ, you cannot draw near to God, you cannot find peace, you cannot be justified, you cannot be sanctified, and you cannot be passed over in judgment. Your works of righteousness, though highly lauded by men, are not sufficient to save you. Without the shedding of blood is no remission. The blood of Christ has been shed and remission is available. But you must apply it to your heart to benefit from its efficacy.

Conclusion

The life of Rahab is typical of the spiritual journey of the believer. She was a sinner. She was under the condemnation of God. She obtained grace. She heard the word of God. She believed in the God of Israel and accepted Him as her God. She was spared the judgment that fell on her city. She was happily married and joined the ancestry of Christ. She was given the sure hope of eternal life. So ends all of God's dealings with those who repent and turn to Him for mercy. The story always ends in graceful redemption, in triumph over evil, and in exaltation to a life of bliss and abundance with the One who loves with genuine and endless love.

Rahab exhorts all men, despite their color, creed, and limitations, to submit to God, believing that He can do for them and their family "exceedingly abundantly above all that we could ask or think," for His grace is no respecter of persons. She assures us that there is no sinful practice too powerful for the strength of divine forgiveness, and there is none so far fallen to be beyond the reach of the extended arms of God, if there is true desire to leave behind the sinful life, and a concurrent determination to live under the Lordship of Christ.

Are you bound by a life of sin from which escape seems impossible? Are you angry because life seems unfair to you by virtue of your color, culture, or upbringing, making you feel like "children of a lesser god?" Then know this: none of these factors matter to God for He is neither limited by them nor influenced by them. God looks on the heart. He said, "to this man will I look: To him that is of a contrite spirit and a broken heart." As far as the world of Jericho was concerned, Rahab was a nobody in whom there is nothing good, a blemish to society, a dishonor to the family, a cheap plaything for dull and senseless men, a soulless life form to be dispensed with after use. They saw her through the eyes of unenlightened men! But God saw a woman who yearned for redemption from the life of sin. He saw a woman who wanted better for herself and her family but did not know where to turn. He saw a woman with a contrite spirit and a broken heart, with a deep yearning for deliverance. In response, God looked her way and Divine providence directed the men of Israel to her home, for whom else but God can vindicate His children sleeping over at the house of a renowned prostitute?

Thus, though you may be despised and rejected by men, know this: God loves you. And it is not by accident this message has come to you, but by Divine design. As God led men to the home of Rahab, so He has directed this communication to you. It is my prayer that you will receive this "messenger" of God, that you will believe in the Lord God of Israel, accept His offer of salvation through Jesus Christ, and allow Him to seal you with His precious blood, the only guarantee you will be spared from the wrath to come on the godless world. Grace has done its work. Now you must do yours. Receive Him and be saved!